Thug Kitchen Party Grub
Copyright © 2015 by Thug Kitchen LLC.

Published by Collins, an imprint of HarperCollins
Publishers Ltd

First Canadian edition

HarperCollins Publishers Ltd
2 Bloor Street East, 20th Floor
Toronto, Ontario, Canada
M4W 1A8

www.harpercollins.ca

Book design by Rae Ann Spitzenberger
Lettering and illustrations by Nick Hensley-Wagner
Photographs by Thug Kitchen

Borders (throughout) by idiz/Shutterstock
Box art (pages ix, 31, 53, 83, 121, 134, 210, 211,
215, 233) by sadragon/Shutterstock
Background (page 170) by donatas/205/
Shutterstock

Library and Archives Canada Cataloguing in
Publication information is available upon request.

ISBN: 9781443445634

Printed in the United States

RRD 9 8 7 6 5 4 3

"A party without a cake is really just a meeting."

—Julia Child

You walk into a party at your friend's place, the crowd is looking right, the playlist is solid, and then you see the spread. There are some empty bags of greasy, broken chips, cans of grey dip and corn-syrup salsa, and a sweaty pile of Vienna sausages. And drinks? Yeah, there's room-temperature beer. How the fuck are you supposed to enjoy yourself when the food and drink situation is saying "meh, whatever"? That shit will not stand anymore.

We're back to show y'all how to PARTY LIKE YOU GIVE A FUCK.

Parties happen way more than you think: birthdays, holidays, graduations, sports shit, block parties, welcome parties, goodbye parties, Mario parties. Whateverthefuck excuse you need to get together with some friends and family to eat some good food is a party in our book and should be treated like one. Don't roll up to our place with a single serving bag of pretzels thinking that's cool.

Come correct or don't come at all.

Parties should be about having a good time; not about eating a bunch of depressing garbage that you're gonna regret tomorrow. Party food usually involves a bunch of prepackaged shit from the store. Which means the nonsense you're eating when you're trying to feel good with friends is loaded with trans fats, artificial everything, and a shitload of sodium. And if you're drinking alcohol on top of all that super-salty food, it's only gonna dehydrate your ass and drag you down more. A great party spread not only tastes good but is filling enough to keep that party rollin' all night after lesser snacks would've let you down. That's why we're here: to keep you from suffering from subpar snacks at your next celebration. Never again.

Out on the road and through various tubes on the Internet, we kept hearing from people that one of the hardest things about starting to eat healthy is hanging out with all the careless motherfuckers/friends who don't give a damn about what they eat. Our last book, *Thug Kitchen: The Official Cookbook,* got you cooking healthy food for yourself at home, but let's be real—that falls apart every time you spend the holidays at a flavorless family function or some work party where all they've got for health-conscious folks are wet baby carrots and limp celery sticks. Ugh, that shit is insulting. This isn't a sixth-grade sack lunch, it's a motherfucking. PARTY. SPREAD. Plenty of people fall off the healthy-eating wagon in social settings, give up, and struggle to start again. That's why we had to come back and help you shake up your snack and party grub game.

You're holding a MOTHERFUCKING BIBLE of tricks, tips, and recipes

that you can bring to any occasion like a BBQ, potluck, fancy dinner, or beer pong tournament without anyone giving you shit for trying to eat better. The only question you'll get will be "why the fuck didn't you make more?" So whether you're the host or a guest, you shouldn't stoop to store-bought solutions.

Let us help you. Showing up to a house party with a basket of raw, unseasoned kale is going to get your ass kicked by even the most passive of hippies, so don't be that person. We've crafted up some tasty grub with affordable, easy-to-find ingredients that anyone will fall in love with, long before they realize they just ate a plateful of healthy, plant-based food.

DIETARY DECEPTION: the most delicious kind.

Maybe you're not the partying type so you think you're getting left out. First off, the minimum attendance for any party is one. You should have the best food and drinks that your loner ass can make while you binge-watch Netflix. If you don't take care of #1, who the hell will? So live it up, you fucking hermit. Secondly, use the badass food in here as an excuse to get out and pretend you're an extrovert. Challenge yourself because hanging out with other humans is actually a healthy habit. Studies have found that people who frequently

interact with other people live longer than the social adverse among us. The health benefits of hanging with other people on the regular can be as obvious as a reduced risk for things like depression, but socializing can also reduce your risk for cardiovascular problems, some cancers, and can even lower your blood pressure. GODDAMN. So like everyone else, you're stressed with work, worried about money, and traffic's got you all fucked up and thus you're never in the mood to go out or see other people. We fucking get it, but you need to get out there. Use this book as a guide so you can show up with a smile and some bombass food, even if you're wearing your sweatpants. Nobody will say a goddamn thing.

Not invited? Throw your own fucking party. If you cook it, they will come. The Beastie Boys fought for your right to party. Don't let that shit be in vain. And we know money is tight but you gotta eat anyway, so you might as well not do it alone. This book is packed with recipes you can use to feed your crew no matter your budget. Serve your squad some tiny portions and call that shit *tapas*. Problem solved.

Before you even ask, no, you can't just have drinks and no food.

Even the DRUNKEST MOTHERFUCKERS get hungry eventually.

And people will get cranky real quick. They'll start digging through your pantry and crunching on uncooked noodles. Save them from themselves. Also, this is the perfect time to show those garbage-eating goats you call friends that healthy food can satisfy their tequila-soaked cravings better than

some greasy shit. Not only will it fill them up, but they won't feel like shit the next day. Don't let them go out and order 16 soft tacos with fire sauce. That's not dinner, that's a ticking-time poo. Curb the late-night drive-thru decisions by serving and eating quality food at the party. Do those deep-fried friends a solid.

And yeah, you're gonna find some decorating ideas tucked away in these pages, but keep your head in check.

The only real VIP at any party is the food.

Nobody is on their way to the party thinking "I hope there are some hand-turned artisanal paper straws and reclaimed wooden cake stands." For fuck's sake. Just be sure to have the food and drinks handled, and then you can worry about party props with what's left in your budget.

Worried that your apartment sucks? Guess what: Everybody is living or has lived in a bleak apartment, so anyone who is talking some silly shit can GTFO because they're at the wrong party. Sure, you might not have enough furniture or whatever, but you can just sit your ass on the floor and call that an indoor picnic.

ADAPT, MOTHERFUCKER.

Just like Martha, we don't accept any excuses in the entertaining game. Thug Kitchen will get your party from "livable" to "legendary" in no time. We've used every waking moment we had over the last year testing these recipes on everyone we could, every chance

we got. That's right, we partied our asses off for you. You're fucking welcome.

As usual, our recipes will meet you wherever you're at. We got stuff in here for new cooks just getting their shit together to hall-of-fame hosts looking to try new things. Even if you do this plant-based shit part-time, you should know how to host people with all kinds of diets. Plant-based meals are an all-inclusive party must that everyone can enjoy. Except for that one cousin of yours but they fucking hate everything so stop trying to make them happy. We got you covered with brunch ideas to badass sides, from casseroles to cocktails. So suit up and sit down because your ass is about to get schooled in how to cook up some good shit worth sharing. You might get some glitter on you—you've been warned.

The book is organized in typical cookbook fashion: by types of dishes. So we've got the breakfast/brunch grub up front, dips and snack shit right after, then your salads, sides, and sauces, entrées (obvs), and bringing up the rear are desserts and booze. If you need help planning your party, we've scattered some legit menus throughout the book so you can get down with minimal planning. If you're freaking out about cooking that many dishes in a short amount of time, then just delegate that shit. Get some friends to cook these meals with you or, better yet, scan the recipe outta this book and send it to them with the note, "Make this for Saturday or don't bother coming." If they're a legit friend they will hop to and if not, go get better friends. When planning out your menu, don't forget to check the number of servings for each recipe, right next to the title. Nothing is worse than starting on dinner and realizing that there's no way in hell you have enough food for everyone. One cup of dip for 10 people ain't gonna fly. If you're cooking on a smaller scale, like for you or some family, we recommend complementary dishes in the brief intro text thingies for many of the recipes, but you do you. Don't feel obligated to take our recommendations; it's not like we wrote the fucking book or anything.

RECIPE RUNDOWN

Do this shit every time you get ready to cook:

» Before you start cooking, read the recipes all the way through so you know exactly what the fuck you're diving into. We cannot stress this shit enough. Read them. ALL. THE. WAY. THROUGH. This will save you at least one panic attack. You might not realize that you need to marinate something for 2 hours if you don't read the recipe and then get really fucked when it comes time to eat and you're still waiting on the food. We've been there and wouldn't recommend it. Don't blame the recipe, blame your damn self.

» Lay out all the pots, spoons, knives, etc., that you're gonna need to whip up the recipe you picked out, because it's a pain in the ass to reach for your mixing bowl when you're like 8 steps deep in the dish and realize you loaned it to your neighbor last summer but never got that shit back.

» Make sure you actually have all the ingredients you need. Last-minute substitutions made in a frenzy usually end up really fucking up a dish and ruining your hard work. Don't come crying to us because you thought it was alright to use applesauce instead of a chopped apple in your cake and it's a soupy mess. Think that shit through and double-check your ingredients list before you start just dumping whatthefuckever into a bowl. You'll end up wasting food and your own damn time otherwise. Up to you, though; maybe you like kitchen drama.

HOW TO DEAL WITH HATERS

You might have noticed that all our recipes are vegan, meaning they don't call for any animal products like cheese, dairy milk, and meat. That doesn't mean you need to be vegan to cook our food though. Maybe you just want to mix up your diet, maybe you realized you haven't eaten any fiber in the last 5 years, or maybe you just like tasty fucking food. Whatever your reason, don't apologize for trying out new shit. What you eat is a deeply personal decision and every motherfucker under the sun likes to offer up their unsolicited opinion about how you should eat. Here are our tips for dealing with some of the dumbass questions you might get if someone notices you're eating a vegetable.

"EWW, I HATE VEGGIES. HOW CAN YOU EAT THAT?" If this is a child, let that shit slide. If this is a grown-ass adult, laugh in their goddamn face. Avoiding veggies isn't really a fucking option. Hate drinking water, too? Tough, you need that shit to live, just like you need fruits and veggies. People who hate on vegetables have probably never had veggies cooked well, so offer them a bite of whatever you're grubbing on.

"BUT LIKE, WHERE DO YOU GET YOUR PROTEIN?" WHY. THE. FUCK. are some people so focused on protein intake but don't give a single flying fuck about all the sodium, sugar, and fat they consume? If you're eating the standard American diet, on average you're consuming more than double your actual protein requirements every year. So just calm the fuck down with that played-out protein bullshit. Beans, legumes, and vegetables are staples of a plant-based diet and many of them contain more protein per calorie than your traditional slab of meat. If the people you're talking to wanna just ignore facts, then just ignore their face.

"AHHH, VEGAN FOOD IS SO BLAND. I HATE IT." Know what else is bland? Underseasoned food. Don't blame plants because some folks don't know how to cook them or use spices, blame the cook, that's on them. We've all had some sad-ass pork chops but you won't hear anyone blaming meat for tasting like packing peanuts. Herbs, spices, hot sauce, BBQ sauce, and marinara are almost always vegan, so people should rethink where to place the blame for flavorless food. *COUGH* THE COOK *COUGH*

The best defense against veggie haters is a plate full of fan-fuckin-tastic food that you brought to share. No need to push a motherfucking agenda at the dinner table. More people will support you and your dietary choices if your decision is for yourself and you don't force that shit on other people. Just share your kickass food and wait for people to start saying shit like "This is pretty good. Can't believe it's vegan." Save your eye roll and just be chill; you were there once, too.

No preaching or soapbox required, just DOPE FOOD and a GOOD ATTITUDE.

BADASS BREAKFASTS AND BOUGIE BRUNCHES

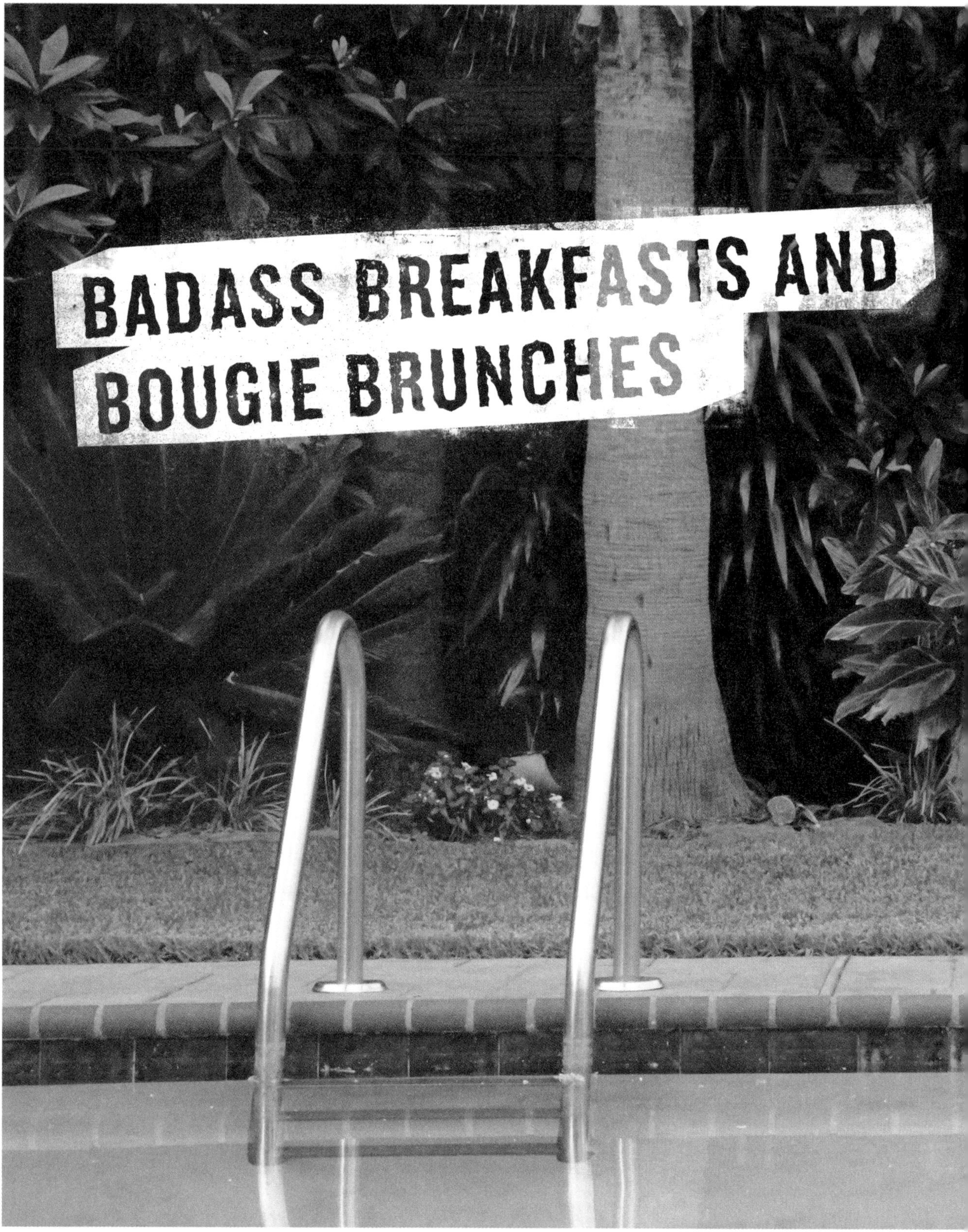

MELON AND MINT
FRUIT SALAD 5

SAVORY GRITS
WITH MIDSUMMER
SUCCOTASH 6

LAZY-MORNING
FRITTATA 8

CINNAMON APRICOT
FRENCH TOAST 9

HOMEMADE TORTILLAS
WITH MIXED FRUIT
COMPOTE 10

GRITS AND SWEET
POTATO BREAKFAST
CASSEROLE 12

SAVORY MINI
WAFFLES 15

PUMPKIN
FRENCH TOAST
CASSEROLE 16

BAKED RICE AND
LEEK CAKES 17

POTATO LEEK
CAKES 20

SAVORY TOMATO
AND NECTARINE
COBBLER 22

COCONUT PANCAKES
WITH MANGO COULIS
24

POPPY SEED PROTEIN
WAFFLES 28

BREAKFAST TEMPEH
AND POTATO TACO
BAR 29

SCRAMBLED CURRY
TOFU FRIED RICE
32

DAMN RIGHT WE GUTTED A MELON
AND FILLED IT WITH OTHER MELON CHUNKS

THAT'S PRETTY FUCKED UP
WHEN YOU THINK ABOUT IT

LOOKS GOOD THOUGH

MELON AND MINT FRUIT SALAD

If you're at a summer picnic, people will be expecting a fruit salad, no question. So roll up with this shit and make everyone else who brought a storebought one look like careless assholes who hate their friends and good food.

2 small melons,*
chopped up into chunks
no bigger than a nickel
(about 10 cups)

¼ teaspoon grated
lemon zest**

½ teaspoon sugar***

1 tablespoon minced
fresh mint

1 Mix the melon, lemon zest, sugar, and mint together in a big ass bowl. Let this chill in the fridge for a minimum of 2 hours, or you can let it hang out overnight. If you're going for the longer chill, leave the mint out until you're ready to serve so that green is still looking all nice and fresh.

2 Serve cold and appreciate how badass melons are.

* We like to do a combo of cantaloupe and honeydew, but use whatever the hell is ripe when you run to the store. All the same melon is chill too if you're super into cantaloupe or whatever.

** So fucking fancy. See page 218 if you are lost.

*** You can leave this sugar out if your melons are just that fucking good, but this shit helps them release a little extra juice and sweetness in case you got one that's doing you dirty.

SAVORY GRITS WITH MIDSUMMER SUCCOTASH

If you're in the mood for a fancy-looking brunch that will actually fill you the fuck up, then look no further. The creamy grits are like a warm blanket for your belly and the succotash will give you all the protein you need to deal with whatever bullshit the day might bring.

Savory Grits (recipe follows)

2 teaspoons olive oil

¼ cup chopped yellow or white onion

1 zucchini, chopped

1 red bell pepper, chopped

1 clove garlic, minced

2 cups shelled edamame or lima beans*

1 cup corn kernels**

¼ cup chopped fresh basil

1 teaspoon lemon juice

¼ teaspoon salt

Toppers: chopped chives, fresh basil, dill

*Lima beans are more traditional, but we like edamame better. We'll leave the decision up to you.

** This is about 1 corncob's worth, but you can get kernels from the freezer if you really fucking have to.

1 Make the savory grits (next page, dumbass) and while they're cooking, make the succotash. Grab a wok or large skillet and warm up the olive oil over medium heat. Add the onion, zucchini, and bell pepper and sauté that shit until the onion starts to look translucent, about 5 minutes.

2 Add the garlic, edamame, and corn and cook for another 3 minutes so everything gets warmed up. Add the basil, lemon juice, and salt. Stir that shit up, then turn off the heat.

3 Serve the grits up right away and top with the succotash and a couple pinches of the fresh herbs.

HOUSE RULES

Edamame are just immature soybeans and tasty as hell. You can find that shit already shelled in the freezer near the peas. Don't accidently grab the shit still in the pods and make a ton of fucking work for yourself. #notworthit

SAVORY GRITS

1 Grab a large pot and bring the broth and milk to a boil over medium heat. Gently whisk in the grits and the salt. Don't just dump all the grits in there and get them all clumpy and fucked up from the start. Bring it all to a boil and then reduce that heat to low. Cover the pot and let that deliciousness simmer for 20 to 30 minutes. Stir the fucker on occasion, because if it gets too hot, its corny ass will stick to the bottom.

2 When the grits have absorbed most of the liquid and are tender, turn off the heat and stir in the nooch.

* Almond milk is fine, use whatever you want.

** Not that instant shit.

*** WTF? See page 231.

3½ cups vegetable broth or water

3 cups unsweetened nondairy milk*

1½ cups stoneground grits**

¼ teaspoon salt

¼ cup nooch***

LAZY-MORNING FRITTATA

1 tablespoon olive oil

1 medium yellow onion, chopped

2 red bell peppers, roasted* and chopped

1½ cups finely chopped broccoli (about the size of chickpeas)

1 cup chopped button or cremini mushrooms

3 cups chopped kale or spinach

3 cloves garlic, minced

½ teaspoon salt

2 teaspoons dried basil

1 teaspoon dried thyme

½ teaspoon dried oregano

Black pepper

1 pound extra-firm tofu, drained

1 cup cooked chickpeas**

½ cup unsweetened nondairy milk

1 tablespoon lemon juice

¾ cup nooch***

1 tomato, sliced into rounds

Spray oil

A frittata is like a savory cake you can munch on all morning while deciding when the fuck you're gonna get in the damn shower. It's okay if you don't, because this frittata loves you no matter what.

1 Warm up your oven to 350°F. Grease up a pie pan or similar-size baking dish.

2 In a large skillet, warm up the oil over medium heat. Add the onion and sauté it around until it starts to brown, 5 to 7 minutes. Add the roasted bell peppers, broccoli, and mushrooms and cook until the mushrooms start releasing their liquid, about 3 minutes. Add the kale, garlic, and salt and cook all of that together until the kale starts to wilt, 3 to 4 more minutes. Add the basil, thyme, oregano, and a dash of black pepper and cook for 1 more minute to warm up the herbs, and then turn the fucking heat off.

3 Throw the tofu, chickpeas, milk, and lemon juice into a blender or food processor and run that shit until it looks sort of smooth. A couple of chickpea chunks are cool, so don't stress. Pour this into the skillet full of veggies, sprinkle in the nooch, and mix it up so everything is combined. Spread this all into the greased pie pan in an even layer, place the tomato slices on top, spray with a little oil, and throw that fucker right in the oven.

4 Bake until it looks set and is kinda golden around the edges, 30 to 40 minutes. Let it sit for about 15 minutes before slicing so it doesn't just fall apart. Cut into slices like a pie and serve warm.

* WTF? See page 217.

** This is about two-thirds of a 15-ounce can of chickpeas. Just save the rest of that shit for a salad or something.

*** WTF? See page 231.

CINNAMON APRICOT FRENCH TOAST

MAKES 6 PIECES
OF FRENCH TOAST,
BUT IT'S EASY AS
HELL TO DOUBLE
OR TRIPLE FOR A
BRUNCH CROWD

This contains some of the dopest shit in life: cinnamon, apricots, and French fucking toast. If you disagree, then clearly you don't appreciate the simple things and you should GTFO of the kitchen.

BATTER

2 cups sweetened vanilla nondairy milk*

¼ cup packed dried apricots**

¼ teaspoon grated orange zest (optional)***

1 tablespoon ground flaxseed or chia seeds

1½ teaspoons nooch****

¼ teaspoon ground cinnamon

Spray oil

½ loaf day-old crusty bread, cut into six ½-inch-thick slices

Maple syrup, cinnamon, and fresh fruit, for serving

1 Make the batter: Grab a small saucepan and dump in the milk and apricots. Let that shit simmer over medium heat for 5 minutes and then let it cool for another 5.

2 Pour the cooled milk/apricot mixture into a blender with the orange zest (if using) and ground flaxseeds. Blend that bitch up until it looks mostly smooth.

3 Pour the batter from the blender into a pie pan or similar-size shallow dish and then slowly stir in the nooch and cinnamon. SLOWLY, GODDAMMIT.

4 Warm a griddle over medium heat and spray a little oil on it so these fuckers won't stick. Soak your bread slices in the batter for a couple seconds on each side and then throw them right on the griddle. Cook until they look golden and tasty all over, 1 to 2 minutes a side. Serve with maple syrup, an extra dash of cinnamon, and some fresh fruit if you're feeling Frenchy.

We use almond, because, well, fuck all the other milks.

** *About 11 quarter-size apricot halves if you really stuff those bastards in there.*

*** *No clue how to zest? See page 218.*

**** *WTF? See page 231.*

HOMEMADE TORTILLAS WITH MIXED FRUIT COMPOTE

TORTILLA DOUGH
2 cups flour (whole wheat pastry, whole wheat, or all-purpose)

½ teaspoon salt

¼ cup olive oil

¾ cup water

1 tablespoon lime juice

FRUIT COMPOTE
3 cups of your favorite fresh or frozen berries* (chopped into bite-size pieces if necessary)

2 tablespoons orange juice

2 tablespoons brown sugar

½ teaspoon vanilla extract (optional)**

Pinch of salt

Serve the warm tortillas with a little coconut oil on the side to smear on if people want.

1 First get going on the tortilla dough: In a medium bowl, mix together the flour, salt, and oil so that you get some pea-size clumps of oil all in that shit. Make a well in the center and pour in the water and lime juice. Mix it all together until there are no more dry spots. Still looking kinda dry? Add up to ¼ cup extra water, 1 tablespoon at a time so you don't fucking overdo it like you always do, until that fucker looks all moist. Shape it into a ball, cover the bowl with some plastic wrap, and stick it in the fridge while you make the compote. Fuck it, you could even do this shit the night before.

2 Now make the fruit compote while that dough chills out: Throw the berries, orange juice, brown sugar, vanilla (if using), and salt into a medium saucepan over a medium-low heat. The berries will start releasing a bunch of liquid soon, so chill the fuck out if you think it looks too dry right now. Bring that shit to a simmer and cook it until the berries start breaking down and the liquid starts to evaporate, 20 to 30 minutes depending on what berries you picked. When it looks like a cross between jam and syrup, remove from the heat and get back to those tortillas. This shit can totally be done the night before too.

3 Grab the dough from the fridge and kinda knead it around in the bowl for a couple minutes. Divide the dough up into 8 to 12 equal portions (depending on how big of a tortilla you want). On a floured surface roll those fuckers out into thin tortilla shapes. You know what you're fucking looking for here. Warm up a skillet or a griddle over a medium-high heat and throw in the first tortilla right now. Cook it for about 30 seconds to 1 minute on each side until it starts getting kinda opaque and toasty looking. Again, you know what the fuck a cooked tortilla looks like. Cook it until it looks like that. These will keep for about 1 week in the fridge.

4 Serve them up warm, and put a big old spoon in the compote.

* Strawberries, blueberries, raspberries, all that shit would be good here. If you are all about that one-berry life, don't add anything else.

** Optional as fuck, but if you have vanilla in the house don't skip it.

GRITS AND SWEET POTATO BREAKFAST CASSEROLE

1 tablespoon olive oil

½ yellow onion, sliced

1½ cups grated raw
sweet potato*

1 medium yellow squash
or zucchini, grated

1 red bell pepper,
chopped

2 cups chopped spinach

2 cloves garlic, minced

1 tablespoon Bragg's,**
soy sauce, or tamari

1 teaspoon paprika

¼ teaspoon chili powder

¼ teaspoon black pepper

1 tablespoon lemon juice

2 teaspoons vinegary hot
sauce, such as Tabasco

1 batch Savory Grits
(page 7)

½ cup unsweetened
nondairy milk

¼ cup nooch**

Whether you're feeding a crowd or making yourself breakfast for a week, this savory son of a bitch is a solid go-to. If you need any more reasons to cook this, here are three: 1. Grits 2. Sweet Potatoes 3. Hot Sauce—need we say more?

1 In a large skillet or wok, heat up the olive oil over medium heat. Add the onion and sauté until it starts to get browned in some spots, 5 to 7 minutes depending on your drafty-ass kitchen. Add the sweet potato, squash, and bell pepper and sauté until the sweet potato starts to soften up, about 5 minutes. Throw in the spinach, garlic, Bragg's, paprika, chili powder, and black pepper and keep on cooking that shit until the spinach wilts down, about 2 minutes. Stir in the lemon juice and hot sauce, then remove from the damn heat. Taste and add more of whateverthefuck you think it's missing. Let that cool while you make the grits or even make this shit the night before and sleep in the extra 30 minutes. You know you want to. (See House Rules on opposite page.)

2 Make the grits just like we say to on page 7. When they are all cooked through, remove from the heat and stir in the sweet potato mixture, the milk, and the extra ¼ cup nooch (the grits already have nooch in them—this is extra).

3 Warm up your oven to 350°F. Grease up a 9 x 13-inch baking dish.

4 Pour that whole mess into the baking dish and bake until the edges look golden and fucking delicious, about 30 minutes. Let it cool for a couple minutes before serving.

5 Serve warm with extra hot sauce on the side.

* This takes about 1 medium sweet potato and is a fucking workout on your arm. If someone in your place owes you a favor, call it in for this shit or borrow their food processor with that fancy grating attachment thing.

** WTF? See page 231.

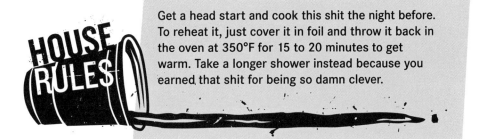

Get a head start and cook this shit the night before. To reheat it, just cover it in foil and throw it back in the oven at 350°F for 15 to 20 minutes to get warm. Take a longer shower instead because you earned that shit for being so damn clever.

PARTY PLAYBOOK
✕✕✕

IT'S BRUNCH, BITCHES

Brunch—because breakfast has come and gone but lunch is just too fucking far away. Seize what's left of your Sunday and wake up your taste buds with some of these dope dishes.

SAVORY MINI WAFFLES

MAKES ABOUT
12 MINI WAFFLES,
DEPENDING ON
HOW YOU POUR
THAT SHIT

WHO THE FUCK SAYS WAFFLES ALWAYS HAVE TO BE SWEET? Whip up these savory sons of bitches and mix up your waffle game.

---

1 Warm up the waffle iron.

2 In a small bowl, mix together the milk and vinegar and set aside.

3 In a large bowl, whisk together the cornmeal, flour, nooch, baking powder, and salt so that they are all mixed.

4 Stir the smoky onions into the milk mixture. Make a well in the center of the flour mixture and add the milk/onion stuff and the oil. Whisk everything together a couple times and then add the chives. Stir a few more times until the chives are all mixed in, there aren't any dry spots, and only a few lumps.

5 Spray the warmed-up waffle iron with some oil so those bitches won't stick, then pour in about ¼ cup of the batter for each waffle section on your iron. Cook until golden brown according to your waffle maker's directions. Serve warm with the dipping sauce.

* Same shit that you'd use to make cornbread, not polenta.

** WTF? See page 231.

2¼ cups unsweetened nondairy milk (your favorite)

1 teaspoon apple cider vinegar or lemon juice

1½ cups finely ground cornmeal*

1 cup all-purpose or whole wheat flour

2 tablespoons nooch**

1 tablespoon baking powder

½ teaspoon salt

Smoky onions (from Cobb Salad, page 104)

2 tablespoons olive oil

2 tablespoons minced chives or green onions

Spray oil

Roasted Garlic Dip (page 88)

1 large crusty loaf of stale bread*

3 tablespoons ground flaxseed

2 cups nondairy milk

½ teaspoon apple cider vinegar or lemon juice

1½ cups canned pumpkin puree**

¼ cup packed brown sugar

1 tablespoon vanilla extract

2 teaspoons ground cinnamon

1 teaspoon ground ginger

½ teaspoon ground nutmeg

⅓ cup nooch***

Spray oil

* We like sourdough, but you could use French or whatever the fuck you've got. You want it to be stale though, so it doesn't get really fucking soggy as it bakes. Eat the fresh stuff and wait until you have some old-ass bread to make this.

** Not pumpkin pie mix; that shit shouldn't exist. Buy a 15-ounce can of plain pumpkin puree (or steam and puree some shit yourself).

*** WTF? See page 231.

PUMPKIN FRENCH TOAST CASSEROLE

You can get your pumpkin fix without ordering it from some fucking coffee shop. With flavors this awesome, why would anyone prefer drinking a latte instead of eating casserole? Casserole over coffee, always. CASSEROLE. OVER. COFFEE. SAY IT, CASSEROLE OVER . . .

1 Heat up the oven to 375°F. Grease a 9 x 13-inch baking dish.

2 Cut up the bread into bite-size pieces about the size of a quarter and throw them into the biggest bowl you've got. You want around 12 cups.

3 In a medium glass, mix together the ground flaxseed, milk, and vinegar and set aside.

4 In a large measuring glass (or blender if you don't mind cleaning that shit), mix together the pumpkin, brown sugar, vanilla, cinnamon, ginger, and nutmeg until it looks smooth. Stir in the milk mixture until everything is all combined. Pour this over the bread until it all looks coated, sprinkle in the nooch, and stir a couple more times so it looks like all that shit is nice and mixed up.

5 Pour the bread mixture into the baking dish in a sort of even layer and spray the top with a little oil. Cover it with foil, and throw that son of a bitch in the oven. Bake for 20 minutes, then take off the foil and bake until the top looks sorta golden, another 15 to 20 minutes. Let it cool for a few minutes before you dish the hot fucker up.

6 Serve warm with maple syrup and some more cinnamon for sprinkling. Baristas got nothing on this shit.

BAKED RICE AND LEEK CAKES

Crispiness on the outside, flavor on the inside. Pack these little fuckers on your baking sheet for a light brunch bite that makes you look like a fucking top chef. Trust.

---

1 Crank up your oven to 425°F. Set a baking sheet aside.

2 Throw the tofu, vinegar, sesame oil, and soy sauce or tamari together in a blender or food processor and run that shit until that beany motherfucker looks smooth.

3 In a large wok or skillet, heat up the grapeseed oil over medium heat. Add the leeks and cook them until they start to look a little translucent, 2 to 3 minutes. Add the chives, ginger, and garlic and cook for another minute, just so everything gets mixed the fuck up. Then remove from the heat.

4 Add the tofu mixture and cooked rice to the pan with the leeks and mix that shit. Add in ¼ cup of the panko and keep mixing until everything is all combined and there aren't any goddamn pockets of rice hiding out and refusing to cooperate.

5 To make the cakes, pour the remaining 1 cup panko onto a plate. Grab about a golf ball's worth of filling and press it into a kind of patty shape. Your hands are gonna get messy, but just fucking deal with it. The mixture will be a little wetter than you think it should be, but you're wrong so just trust the method and move the fuck on. Coat the patty with the panko by gently pressing it into the crumbs, then place it on the baking sheet.

(continued)

12 ounces extra-firm silken tofu*

1 tablespoon rice vinegar

1 tablespoon toasted sesame oil

1 tablespoon soy sauce or tamari

1 teaspoon neutral oil, such as grapeseed

2 cups diced leeks**

½ cup minced chives or green onions

1 tablespoon minced fresh ginger

2 cloves garlic, minced

2½ cups cooked short-grain white or brown rice***

1¼ cups panko bread crumbs****

Spray oil

Sweet Sesame Teriyaki-Style Sauce (page 18)

* WTF? See page 231.

** See House Rules on page 19.

*** This could be leftover rice or freshly made, it's not going to fucking matter. No clue how to make rice at home because you grew up with that Minute shit? See page 212.

**** WTF? See page 231 if you are confused.

TROUBLE WITH CHOPSTICKS?
FORK THAT SHIT

6 Keep going until you've run out of patties. Ya know, the obvious place to stop. Spray them all lightly with a little oil and bake, turning them halfway, until both sides are golden, about 30 minutes. Serve with the dipping sauce on the side.

SWEET SESAME TERIYAKI-STYLE SAUCE

MAKES ABOUT
1 CUP

1 In a small saucepan, mix together the soy sauce or tamari, broth, orange juice, vinegar, sweetener, sesame oil, ginger, and garlic and stir over medium-low heat.

2 In a small glass, mix together the cornstarch and water until the starch dissolves and isn't clumpy as fuck. Stir that into the saucepan and bring it all to a low simmer until the sauce starts to thicken up, about 2 minutes. Remove from the heat, stir in the sesame seeds if you want, and let that fucker cool.

3 Store it in the fridge and that tasty son of a bitch will keep for 1 week.

* Optional, but they class up the joint.

½ cup soy sauce or tamari

¼ cup vegetable broth

¼ cup orange juice

2 tablespoons rice vinegar

2 teaspoons of your favorite liquid sweetener, such as agave or maple syrup

1 tablespoon toasted sesame oil

1 tablespoon minced fresh ginger

1 clove garlic, minced

2 teaspoons cornstarch or arrowroot powder

1 tablespoon water

2 tablespoons sesame seeds (optional)*

HOUSE RULES

Leeks grow in sandy soil, so when you buy them, they're usually dirty as fuck. To get them clean, dice them up, throw them in a bowl of water, and mix them around so that all the dirt comes loose and sinks to the bottom. Drain and rinse a couple more times so you aren't grinding on some grit with dinner.

POTATO LEEK CAKES

These crispy motherfuckers are baked, not fried, so you can get down on these spectacular spuds without guilt.

2½ cups grated potatoes
(about 1 pound)

1 cup leek strips
(about 1 leek)*

1 cup mashed cooked
navy beans**

2 cloves garlic, minced

2 tablespoons nooch***

2 tablespoons olive oil

½ teaspoon salt

Spray oil

DIPPING SAUCE

½ cup vegetable broth

½ cup unsweetened plain
nondairy milk

½ cup cooked navy
beans**

¼ cup all-purpose flour

1 clove garlic, minced

½ teaspoon Dijon
mustard

2 tablespoons nooch***

1 tablespoon lemon juice

1 teaspoon soy sauce or
tamari

2 tablespoons chopped
fresh dill or chives
(your call)

1 Crank up your oven up to 400°F. Grab a rimmed baking sheet and line it with some parchment paper.

2 In a large bowl, mix the potatoes, leek strips, beans, garlic, nooch, olive oil, and salt and mix all the shit around until you can kinda form little patties.

3 Grab a small handful of that potato mess. Make a thin patty by kinda flattening that shit out as you place it on the baking sheet. Repeat, then spray with a little oil. Bake until those fuckers look golden, about 30 minutes, flipping halfway. While they're crisping up in the oven, your multitasking ass has time to make the sauce.

4 To make the dipping sauce: Throw the broth, milk, beans, flour, garlic, mustard, nooch, lemon juice, and soy sauce or tamari in a blender and run that loud motherfucker until the beans have gone and disappeared.

5 Pour that mixture into a small saucepan and bring it to a gentle simmer, like a couple bubbles, over medium heat. Simmer until the sauce starts thickening up, 3 to 5 minutes. You want that shit to look like you could actually dip something in it, so get it that thick. Remove from the heat and stir in the dill. Taste and add more garlic or whatever you're feeling at that moment.

6 Serve both the sauce and cakes warm.

* See House Rules on page 19.

** One 15-ounce can of beans equals 1½ cups, just what is needed for the cakes and sauce; so yeah, we got your lazy ass like that.

*** WTF? See page 231.

SPEND YOUR
WEEKEND

GETTING
BAKED
NOT FRIED

SAVORY TOMATO AND NECTARINE COBBLER

1 pound nectarines
(about 3 fist-size ones)

1 pound cherry or grape
tomatoes

1 tablespoon cornstarch
or arrowroot powder

2 teaspoons olive oil

½ yellow onion, cut into
thin strips

3 cloves garlic, minced

½ cup chopped fresh
basil

2 teaspoons balsamic
vinegar

¼ teaspoon salt

**CORNMEAL BISCUIT
TOPPING**

1 cup unsweetened
nondairy milk

½ teaspoon apple cider
vinegar or lemon juice

2 cups whole wheat
pastry* or all-purpose
flour

½ cup cornmeal**

1 tablespoon baking
powder

1 tablespoon sugar

½ teaspoon salt

¼ cup refined coconut
oil, well chilled***

Spray oil

In the summertime, tomatoes and nectarines are not only cheap as fuck but in their prime. So grab some of those bastards at the store and cook up this cobbler. Serve alongside a Big-Ass Salad Bowl (page 91) and you've got yourself a brunch worth bragging about.

_____

1 Crank up the oven to 375°F. Grab a 9 x 13-inch or similar-size baking dish.

2 Chop the nectarines up into pieces about the size of a dime and throw them into a medium bowl. You want about 2 cups. Keep that skin on unless you hate flavor, fiber, and yourself, because those fuckers are hard to peel. If your tomatoes are smaller than a dime, you can keep those fuckers whole; otherwise halve them and toss in with the nectarines. Toss them all together with the cornstarch and let it sit for a sec.

3 In a skillet, heat the oil over medium heat. Add the onion and sauté until it looks golden, about 5 minutes. Turn off the heat and add the garlic and nectarine/tomato mixture. Fold in the basil, vinegar, and salt and mix until everything is coated. Toss that into your baking dish and put it all in the oven for 15 minutes while you make the topping.

4 Make the cornmeal biscuit topping: In a small glass, mix up the milk and vinegar and let it sit. In a medium bowl, whisk together the flour, cornmeal, baking powder, sugar, and salt. Crumble the chilled coconut oil into the flour and break into pieces smaller than a pea using a fork or pastry cutter. Make a well in the center and pour in the milk mixture. Stir until a shaggy dough is formed but be careful not to overmix because then you will have some tough biscuits. If it is too dry to stick together, add a tablespoon or two of milk.

5 Turn the dough out on a floured surface and pat it into a roughly 8 x 6-inch rectangle about 1½ inches thick. Using a glass, small bowl, or biscuit cutter, cut out all the motherfucking biscuits you can. You should end up with about 8 if you push all the scraps back together and recut that shit. (If you want this shit to look rustic or you want a lazy option, just spoon that dough into big blobs all over the top of the filling. Done.)

6 After the filling has been in the oven for 15 minutes, lay the biscuits down over it (or in blobs if that's what you're doing). Spray the dough with some oil and stick it back in the oven until the tops of the biscuits look golden and cooked through, 20 to 30 minutes.

7 Let this fucker cool for about 5 to 10 before serving because that fruit filling is crazy-hot straight out of the oven. RIP taste buds. RIP.

* Whole wheat pastry flour is really similar to all-purpose flour in texture and taste but contains all the good bran and germ stuff like you find in whole wheat flour. Basically, it's the shit.

** The finely ground shit you would grab to make cornbread, not the coarse stuff you'd make polenta with.

*** The coconut oil needs to be all white and thick like butter. If it is all runny because it is hot outside, that won't fucking work. Stick it in the fridge until it gets its act together.

MAKES ABOUT
12 REASONABLY
SIZED PANCAKES,
UNLESS YOU'RE
POURING THE
BATTER LIKE A
GODDAMN ROOKIE

COCONUT PANCAKES WITH MANGO COULIS

MANGO COULIS
2 mangoes, cut into cubes*

2 to 4 tablespoons sugar**

1½ teaspoons lemon juice

PANCAKES
2¼ cups sweetened vanilla nondairy milk or coconut milk

½ teaspoon lemon juice or apple cider vinegar

1 tablespoon ground flaxseed

2 cups whole wheat pastry flour, all-purpose flour, or a mix

½ cup shredded coconut, toasted***

3 tablespoons brown sugar

2 teaspoons baking soda

⅛ teaspoon salt

Spray oil

Toppings: fresh-cut fruit, like bananas, strawberries, or extra mangos; a smear of coconut oil

Coulis is just a fancy way of saying fruit puree, so stop freaking the fuck out. You've got this. Plus, pancakes are the hero you need against that hangover you worked up all night. Not every superhero wears capes, some wear coulis.

1 To make the coulis: Throw everything in a food processor or blender and let that fucker run until it's nice and smooth. Pour it into a container and stick it in the fridge until the pancakes are ready. This will keep for a couple days so make this shit ahead of time and get it out of the way.

2 Make the pancakes: In a medium glass, mix together the milk, lemon juice, and ground flax and then set that shit aside.

3 In a big bowl, whisk together the flour, coconut, brown sugar, baking soda, and salt. Make a crater in the middle of the dry mix and pour in the milk. Mix that all together until there are no more dry spots but don't go crazy. Mixing it too much will make your pancakes tough, so try and just chill. No need to start your day off with a pancake panic attack.

(continued)

Party All Night
Cakes

4 Now, you probably know what to do when it comes to cooking up some pancakes, but in case this is your first time doing this shit yourself, keep reading. Grab a skillet or griddle and warm it over medium heat. Lightly grease the pan with some spray oil and pour some pancake batter onto the griddle for each pancake you want. Cook the first side until bubbles appear on top, 2 to 3 minutes. The bubbles mean your pancake has cooked through. Flip and cook the other side until it turns golden brown, 1 to 2 minutes longer.

5 Serve warm, spread with a little coconut oil and with mango coulis all over and some fresh fruit on the side. Sprinkle on some extra toasted coconut if you want people to know exactly how you like to get your day started.

* Can't find a ripe mango? Don't fucking stress. Thawed frozen mango (2 cups) works good too.

** If your mango is superripe and delicious, you might not need any sugar, as the amount to use is directly correlated to the shittiness of your mango. Taste and you'll fucking know what to do.

*** Grab the unsweetened coconut, not that supergross sugary shit. To toast it, just throw it in a small skillet over medium-low heat and stir it around until it starts to look sorta golden and smell nice and nutty. Fucking done. Can't find any shredded coconut? Just leave that shit out and add ½ cup of flour instead.

HOUSE RULES

When figuring out your party budget, know that food comes before décor. Always. Understand that shit? ALWAYS. No one gives a flying fuck about your multicolored streamers when they're starving. WE CAN'T FUCKING EAT GLITTER, JULIE!

BADASS
BREAKFAST IN BED

Anniversary? Birthday? Day off? Sunday? Whatever occasion you're using to guilt someone else into bringing you some big-ass breakfast while you're still lounging in bed, this menu is for you. Of course you could cook this for yourself, then climb back into bed like someone else did all the hard work—that's not all crazy and pathetic or anything.

» **ROASTED POTATOES WITH RED PEPPER DIPPING SAUCE** (page 51)

» **MELON AND MINT FRUIT SALAD** (page 5) or **BOOZY WATERMELON AND PAPAYA SALAD** (page 103)

» **POPPY SEED PROTEIN WAFFLES** (page 28)

» **PIÑA COLADA ICEES** (page 190, sans booze if you're worried about what the neighbors would say)

POPPY SEED PROTEIN WAFFLES

12 ounces soft silken tofu

1½ cups nondairy milk, such as almond

1 tablespoon vanilla extract

Grated zest* of 1 lemon (about 1 tablespoon)

2 tablespoons lemon juice

2 cups all-purpose or whole wheat pastry flour

¼ cup sugar

2 teaspoons baking powder

1 teaspoon baking soda

½ teaspoon salt

2 tablespoons poppy seeds**

Spray oil

Maple syrup, seasonal fruit

Love poppy seed muffins? Love your protein? These waffles got your back. And the extra protein will make you feel as good as these motherfuckers taste. Bonus: Using a blender makes your waffles supersmooth and will wake up all the lazy fuckers in your place, because there's no such thing as a quiet blender.

_____

1 Warm up the waffle iron.

2 In a small blender, mix together the tofu, milk, vanilla, lemon zest, and lemon juice and run that shit until everything is mixed up and looking smooth.

3 In a large bowl, whisk together the flour, sugar, baking powder, baking soda, and salt so that they're all mixed up. Make a well in the center and add the tofu/milk mixture. Whisk everything together until it is just kinda starting to combine and then fold in the poppy seeds. Keep mixing until there aren't any more dry spots and only a few lumps, no need to go crazy.

4 Spray the warmed-up waffle iron with some oil so those bitches won't stick, then pour in some batter. Cook until golden brown according to your waffle maker's directions. Cover with maple syrup, whatever fruit that's in season, and serve hot. Then make those lazy bastards we mentioned earlier clean up the kitchen.

No clue on how to do this zest shit? See page 218.

** Not required but the waffles are way better with them.*

BREAKFAST TEMPEH AND POTATO TACO BAR

Breakfast tacos are a legit brunch choice because you can just throw that shit out on the table and let people assemble them howeverthefuck they like. Your friends don't like tacos before 12 p.m.? Get some new fucking friends.

1 pound small yellow or red potatoes

8 ounces tempeh*

1 large red bell pepper

½ yellow onion

¼ cup vegetable broth or water

2 teaspoons olive oil

1 tablespoon lime juice

2 cloves garlic, minced

1 tablespoon chili powder

1 teaspoon paprika

½ teaspoon ground cumin

½ teaspoon salt

8 to 10 corn or flour tortillas, warmed

Toppings: salsa, hot sauce, shredded lettuce, avocado slices or guacamole, cilantro, lime wedges, jalapeño slices

---

1 Warm up your oven to 400°F. Grab a 9 by 13-inch baking pan, like what you might use for lasagna, and set it aside.

2 Chop up the potatoes (yes, leave the fucking skin on) about the size of your thumbnail. Do the same damn thing with the tempeh, bell pepper, and onion.

3 In a large bowl, mix together the broth, oil, lime juice, garlic, spices, and salt. Add the chopped veggies and tempeh to the bowl and stir it all up until everything is coated with flavor. Throw it all into the baking pan, yes including the liquid, cover it with foil, and bake for 20 minutes.

4 Once it's been braising for about 20 minutes, take off the foil, stir, and bake until the potatoes are soft and the tempeh looks kinda golden, about 25 minutes longer.

5 Serve it up with some warm tortillas and whateverthehell toppings you like in tacos.

WTF? See page 231.

1. **Breakfast Tempeh and Potato Taco** (page 29)

2. **Everyday Guacamole** (page 67)

3. **Lights Out Bloody Mary** (page 209)

4. **Tiny-Ass Hat**

SCRAMBLED CURRY TOFU FRIED RICE

A little bit tofu scramble, a little bit fried rice, this bitch is all delicious. Scared to try savory shit in the morning? Conquer your fears and make this dish and see what you've been missing.

VEGETABLES
1 teaspoon refined coconut or olive oil

2 carrots, chopped

1 red bell pepper, chopped

½ yellow onion, chopped

3 cups chopped spinach*

1 cup green peas**

SCRAMBLED CURRY TOFU
2 teaspoons refined coconut or olive oil

16 ounces extra-firm tofu

1 teaspoon soy sauce or tamari

2 teaspoons yellow curry powder***

2 cloves garlic, minced

¼ cup nooch****

FRIED RICE
2 teaspoons refined coconut or olive oil

4 cups leftover cooked short-grain brown rice

2 teaspoons soy sauce or tamari

1 teaspoon toasted sesame oil

Squeeze of lime or lemon juice

⅓ cup chopped green onions or chives, for serving

1 Stir-fry the vegetables: In a large wok or skillet, heat the oil over medium heat. Add the carrots, bell pepper, and onion and stir-fry those crunchy sons of bitches around until the onion starts to look sorta translucent and the veggies are softening up, like 3 to 4 minutes. Throw in the spinach and green peas and keep cooking until the spinach starts to wilt, another 2 to 3 minutes. Remove from the heat and scrape all that shit onto a plate so you can reuse that pan. Yeah, we hate getting a bunch of pans dirty because dishes are the worst.

2 Now for the scrambled tofu: In the same pan, heat up the oil over medium heat. While that is heating up, drain the tofu and squeeze out as much water as possible. You can squeeze this shit with your hands, no need to press this because again: Fuck extra dishes. Now crumble the tofu into the pan in chunks about the size of a quarter. Some small bits are cool, but the more you stir it, the more shit is gonna break down, so start bigger and let it get smaller on its own. Stir the tofu around until it starts to brown a little, 2 to 3 minutes.

3 Add the soy sauce or tamari, curry powder, and garlic and keep cooking that shit until the tofu is all nice and coated and looking less wet and gushy. You know what the fuck we mean. That should take 2 to 3 minutes longer. Then add the nooch, stir to coat, and remove from the heat. Scrape that shit out onto a plate because that pan has one last job.

4 Make the fried rice: Heat the wok back up over medium heat and add the oil. Throw in the rice and stir-fry until it begins to warm, 3 to 5 minutes. Pour the soy sauce or tamari over the rice, mix well, and then add the cooked vegetables from earlier. Stir-fry for a minute so everything is well mixed. Fold in the scrambled tofu. Pour the sesame oil and lime juice over the pan, stir one more time, and remove from the heat.

5 Top with the green onions and enjoy the fuck out of your savory brunch.

* You could use kale or whatever your go-to green is. No need to buy a bunch of different shit.

** Frozen peas are legit here. Don't overthink this.

*** Do yourself a favor and don't buy any curry powder with salt as an ingredient. You don't need them sneaking extra sodium on you like that.

**** WTF? See page 231.

HOUSE RULES

DON'T EVEN FUCKING THINK about using freshly cooked rice here because it will get all mushy and taste like a disaster. The trick to good fried rice is using cold, leftover cooked rice because it's drier and the rice kernels are separated. This keeps it from being a sticky gross paste, SO PLAN AHEAD.

PRE-PARTY LIKE A FUCKING CHAMP

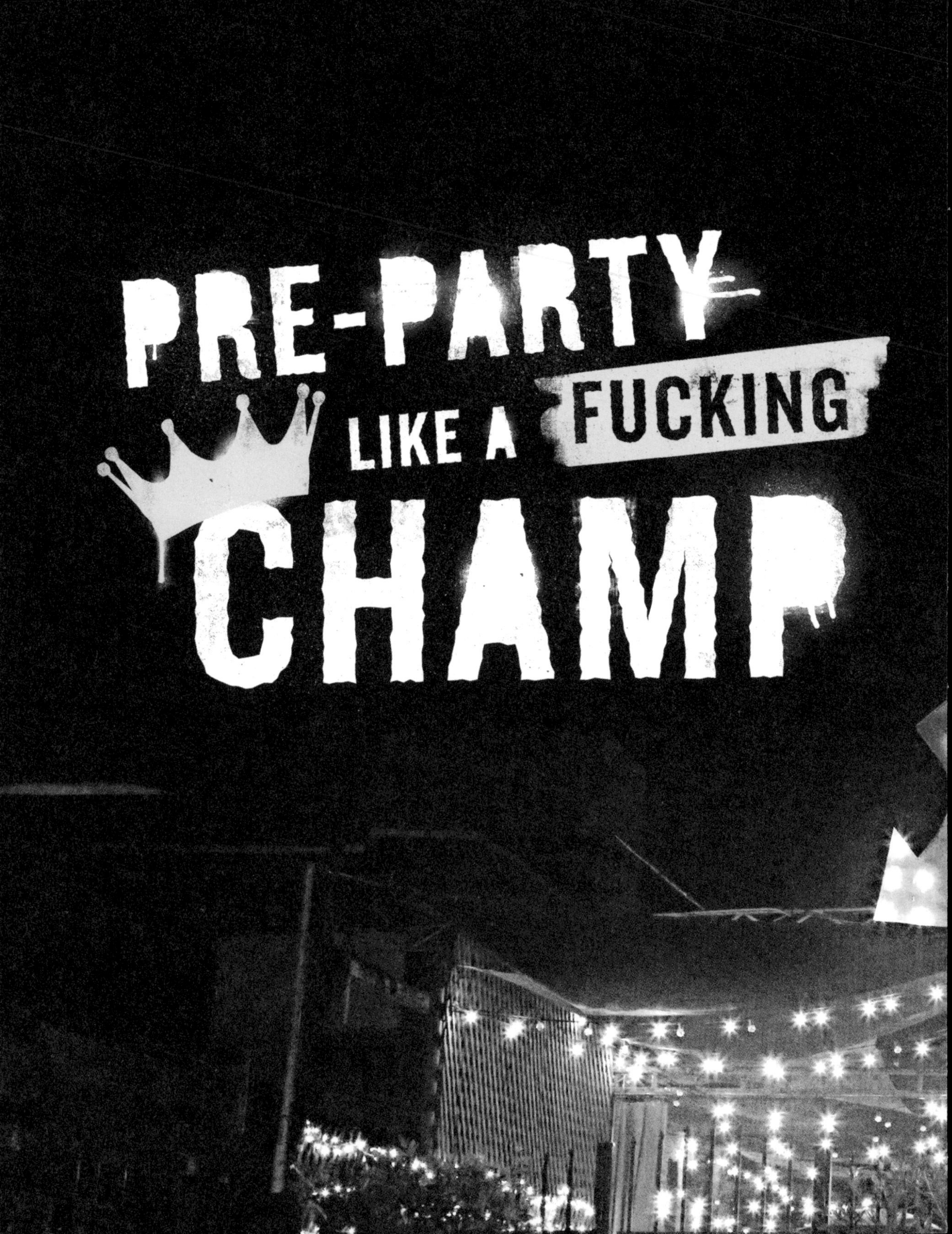

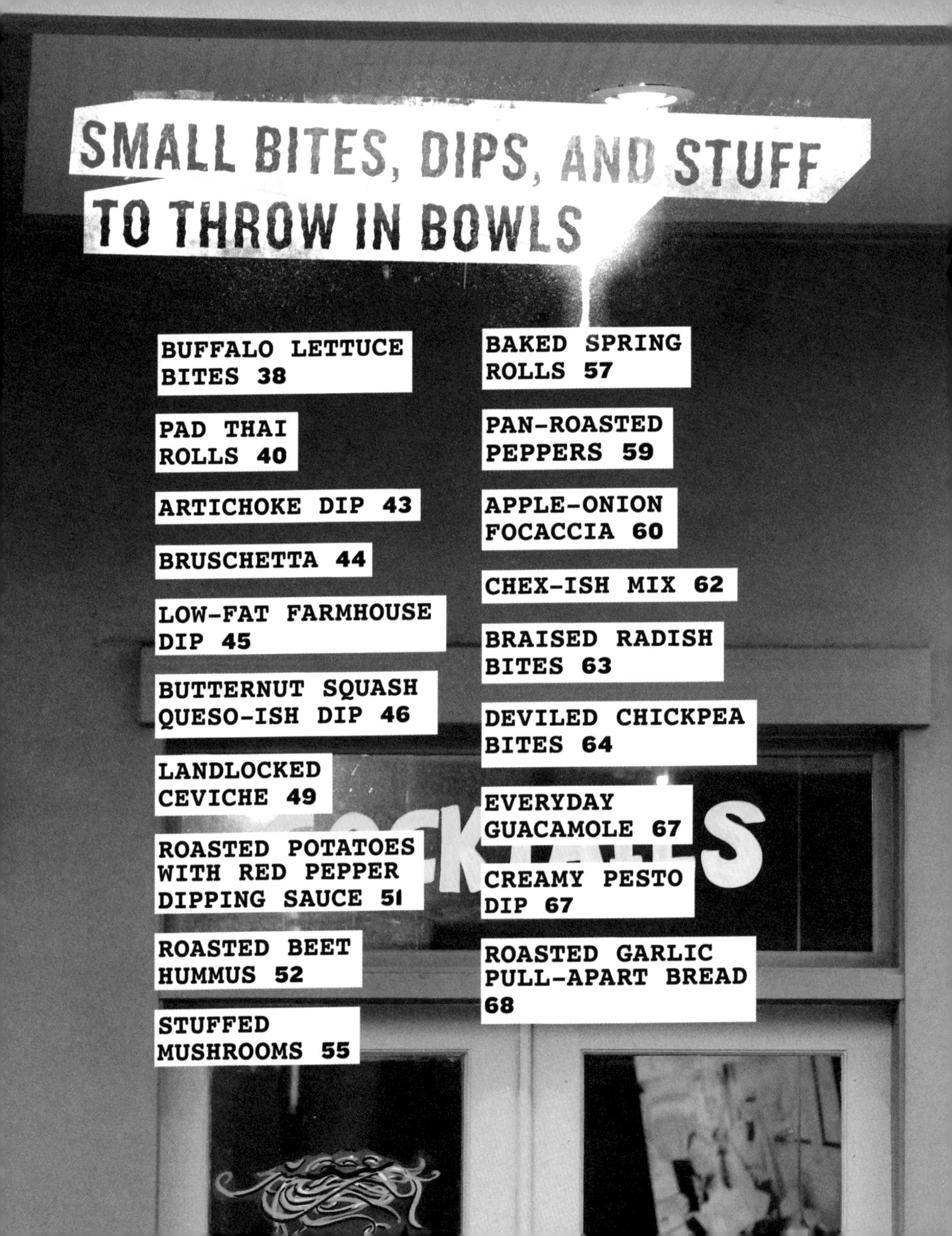

SMALL BITES, DIPS, AND STUFF TO THROW IN BOWLS

BUFFALO LETTUCE BITES 38

PAD THAI ROLLS 40

ARTICHOKE DIP 43

BRUSCHETTA 44

LOW-FAT FARMHOUSE DIP 45

BUTTERNUT SQUASH QUESO-ISH DIP 46

LANDLOCKED CEVICHE 49

ROASTED POTATOES WITH RED PEPPER DIPPING SAUCE 51

ROASTED BEET HUMMUS 52

STUFFED MUSHROOMS 55

BAKED SPRING ROLLS 57

PAN-ROASTED PEPPERS 59

APPLE-ONION FOCACCIA 60

CHEX-ISH MIX 62

BRAISED RADISH BITES 63

DEVILED CHICKPEA BITES 64

EVERYDAY GUACAMOLE 67

CREAMY PESTO DIP 67

ROASTED GARLIC PULL-APART BREAD 68

3 cups cooked chickpeas*

3 ribs celery, chopped (about 1 cup)

1 carrot, shredded (about ½ cup)

¼ cup chopped red onion

1 clove garlic, minced

1 tablespoon lemon juice

2 teaspoons red wine vinegar

2 teaspoons olive oil

¼ teaspoon salt

¼ teaspoon black pepper

2 heads of romaine, butter, or green leaf lettuce, something that can hold a scoop

Buffalo Sauce (opposite), for serving

BUFFALO LETTUCE BITES

Don't worry, vegans, no buffalo or chickens were harmed in the making of these bites. So if that is the only reason you haven't made this shit yet then you are out of fucking reasons.

1 Dump the chickpeas in a food processor and run that shit until they're nice and chopped up. Don't have a processor or don't want to get it dirty? Just throw those beany bastards into a bowl and mash them up with a potato masher or fork. Either way, you don't want any large chunks, but you got some texture; think rice-size chunks for most of it. Dump the mashed chickpeas into a big bowl (if you didn't mash them in one to begin with). Throw in the celery, carrot, red onion, garlic, lemon juice, red wine vinegar, olive oil, salt, and pepper and stir that shit up. Taste and adjust the seasoning how you like. Filling done.

2 To serve, just scoop up some filling into the lettuce leaves. Either spoon some Buffalo sauce over them or set the sauce to the side so your weak-ass friends can control how much heat they eat.

* Two 15-ounce cans, drained and rinsed, are legit too.

BUFFALO SAUCE

Grab a small saucepot and warm up the oil over a medium heat. Add the flour and stir that shit up until it starts smelling nutty, about 2 minutes. Whisk in the broth. It will start looking like gross Play-Doh, but keep going. Slowly whisk in the hot sauce and cider vinegar to keep it from getting chunky. Simmer until the sauce starts to thicken up, 2 to 5 minutes, then remove from the heat.

* Frank's RedHot is traditional, but do whatever basic vinegar red hot sauce you can find at the store.

MAKES ABOUT 1½ CUPS

2 tablespoons olive oil

2 tablespoons all-purpose or whole wheat flour

½ cup vegetable broth

1 cup hot sauce*

1 tablespoon apple cider vinegar or lemon juice

SERVE A SNACK AS GOOD AS YOUR SHIT TALK

**PAD THAI
DIPPING SAUCE**
½ cup seasoned rice vinegar

2 tablespoons sugar

2 teaspoons tomato paste

2 teaspoons chili garlic paste*

1 teaspoon lime juice

½ cup chopped peanuts

FILLING
1 package (6.75 ounces) maifun, glass noodles,** or thin rice noodles

1½ teaspoons soy sauce or tamari

1 teaspoon toasted sesame oil

2 cups thinly sliced red or green cabbage

1 cucumber, cut into very thin sticks

1 package large spring roll wrappers/rice paper wrappers***

1 carrot, cut into very thin sticks

1 cup thickly sliced fresh herbs****

PAD THAI ROLLS

Want pad thai but also want to eat with your hands? We've got your fucking back with way less sodium than that takeout shit. Like all food in wraps, this dish is pretty fucking flexible when it comes to fillings, so feel free to use what you have. Just make sure that you have some other hearty green, something crunchy, and at least one of the herbs. Don't wanna make the tofu? Just leave that shit out.

---

1 For the dipping sauce: Throw the vinegar and sugar into a small saucepot and bring it to a simmer over a medium heat. Let that cook for about 4 minutes, stirring occasionally. Stir in the tomato paste, chili paste, and lime juice and remove from the heat. Once it cools for a couple minutes, pour that shit into a small glass and stick it in the fridge. Don't throw the peanuts on there until right before you serve it otherwise they get all fucking soggy.

2 For the filling: Cook the noodles according to package directions. When they are done, drain them and run them under cold water until they are cool to the touch. Throw them in a medium bowl and toss them up with the soy sauce or tamari and sesame oil. Set aside.

3 Now you should chop up all your veggies into strips about 2 inches long.

4 It's time to wrap this shit up. Warm about 3 inches of water in a wok or skillet over a low heat. You want the water hot but not so hot you can't put your hand in it because that's exactly what you're about to do. Remove from the heat. Place one spring roll wrapper flat in the water for 10 to 15 seconds until it becomes bendy like a noodle. Let the extra water drip off and lay that translucent motherfucker down on a plate.

5 Now you're going to treat this shit like it's a tiny burrito. About ½ inch from the wrapper edge closest to you, lay down the cabbage, cucumber, carrot, herbs, and a forkful of the noodles. Roll that shit over once away from you, then fold the edges in toward the center so you kinda have a rectangle shape going on, and then burrito away. Continue rolling kinda tightly and press the end flap gently against the roll (like the rolls on page 58). Keep making rolls until you run out of filling. If you make these a few hours ahead of time, store them in the fridge with a lightly damp paper towel or clean dish towel over them so their delicate asses don't dry out.

6 To serve, add the chopped peanuts to the top of the dipping sauce and go to town. Finished rolls will keep in the fridge for about 2 days, but if you haven't eaten them by then, you're fucking crazy.

* You can find chili garlic paste by the soy sauce in the store.

** WTF are glass noodles? See page 214.

*** Spring roll or rice paper wrappers look like a stack of chalk-colored, paper frisbee things. They are usually near the soy sauce at the store and are cheap as hell.

**** A combo of cilantro, mint, and basil is legit, but use what you can find.

A DIP SO OLD SCHOOL
THE TUPPERWARE
SHOULD BE A
FUCKING INGREDIENT

ARTICHOKE DIP

This dip has been a staple of parties, Tupperware or otherwise, since they found a way to throw artichokes in a can. Since these canned motherfuckers are available year-round, unlike their full-grown, more fibrous older brothers, there's no reason not to whip up a batch of this low-fat snack. Serve it up with sliced bread, pita, carrot sticks, whatever your favorite dip device is.

¼ medium white onion, chopped

3 cloves garlic

½ cup unsweetened plain nondairy milk

1½ teaspoons soy sauce, tamari, or Bragg's*

¼ cup sliced almonds

1 can (14 ounces) water-packed artichoke hearts, drained and rinsed

2 tablespoons flour**

2 tablespoons olive oil

½ cup vegetable broth

1 cup chopped fresh spinach

¼ cup nooch*

1 tablespoon lemon juice

1 In a blender or food processor, combine the onion, garlic, milk, and soy sauce and pulse that shit until it looks like paste. Add the almonds and pulse again until there aren't any big pieces in there. Add the artichokes and pulse again until it starts to resemble what dip should look like. We prefer it kinda chunky, but if you like it smooth just run it a bit longer.

2 In a small saucepan over medium heat, stir the oil and flour around until it starts to look kinda toasted and smells nutty, about 2 minutes. Yeah, that's right, we're.making.a.motherfucking.roux. Gently whisk in the broth. It's gonna get really thick and Play-Doh looking, just go with it. Add the artichoke mixture and spinach. Keep stirring until everything starts to thicken up and the spinach wilts, about 3 minutes.

3 Add the nooch and lemon juice and heat for another minute. Remove from the heat and taste. Add more lemon juice, garlic, whatever the fuck you think it needs to get it right where you like it.

4 Serve it warm or at room temperature with your favorite dip transportation device.

* WTF? See page 231.

** This can be all-purpose or whole wheat. It doesn't really fucking matter.

BRUSCHETTA

5 fist-size tomatoes, chopped* (about 2½ cups)

¼ cup chopped fresh basil (10 to 12 leaves)

2 teaspoons lemon juice

2 teaspoons balsamic vinegar

2 teaspoons olive oil

⅛ teaspoon salt

1 clove garlic, minced

Crusty bread slices, toasted

If you're unfamiliar with this staple snack, where the fuck have you been? It's basically Italian salsa served on top of carbs. Yeah, everybody fucks with that no matter how you pronounce it.

1 Mix all that shit together (except the bread, dumbass) in a medium bowl and let it chill in the fridge for 30 minutes so all the flavors can hang out and get to know each other. Taste and then add more of what you think it needs. You do you.

2 Serve in a bowl surrounded by the toasted bread or prescoop that shit onto the toasts and pass it around like a bunch of tiny open-faced sammies. Both ways are equally fucking delicious.

* To keep this from being too watery, slice the tomatoes in half lengthwise before you get chopping and use a spoon to kinda scoop out all their seeds and guts. That drippy shit brings no flavor to the party. Stop holding yourself to watery standards. You're better than that.

HOUSE RULES

Ready to leave the party but don't want to say bye to 30 different fucking people? DON'T. Just say "I'll be right back" and then never come back. By the time anyone realizes you're gone, you're chillin' at home with your real friends: sweatpants.

LOW-FAT FARMHOUSE DIP

MAKES ABOUT
1½ CUPS, ENOUGH
FOR 6 TO 8 PEOPLE

This protein-packed dip has all of that ranch taste without any of that sneaky valley bullshit. Save that sad-ass packet of mix for some kind of escalating series of dares later on tonight. That's where it belongs.

- 12 ounces soft silken tofu*
- 2 tablespoons minced shallot or white onion
- 1 clove garlic
- 1 tablespoon apple cider vinegar or white wine vinegar
- 1 tablespoon each minced chives, dill, and parsley
- ½ teaspoon salt
- ½ teaspoon garlic powder**

1 Throw the tofu, shallot, and garlic into a blender or food processor and run until it looks all smooth. Throw in the rest of the ingredients and pulse it a couple of times so everything gets chopped up and mixed in but the herbs are still kinda visible.

2 Let it sit in the fridge at least 1 hour before serving so that the flavors can get to know each other. Serve with whatever vegetables you like and get to dipping. It will keep for 3 to 4 days in the fridge.

WANT TO MAKE IT A DRESSING?

Just add 2 tablespoons of unsweetened plain almond milk to the blender to make it easier to pour later. Fucking done.

WTF? See page 231.

*** We know it's strange to call for two kinds of garlic, but there's a good goddamn reason. This helps give it that store-bought ranch taste that you grew up with. Trust us.*

BUTTERNUT SQUASH QUESO-ISH DIP

1½ cups butternut squash puree*

½ cup diced yellow onion

3 tablespoons all-purpose or whole wheat flour

1½ teaspoons ground cumin

1 teaspoon chili powder

1 teaspoon smoked paprika

3 tablespoons olive oil

½ cup vegetable broth or water

1 cup diced tomatoes with their juices**

¼ cup nooch***

2 cloves garlic, minced

1 or 2 jalapeños, minced

1 tablespoon lime juice

½ teaspoon salt

This dip is so damn tasty that you'll forget that it's full of squash and not a shitload of questionable cheese-like products. Make a double or triple batch because this always disappears fast. You'll get invited to every fucking party ever if you start showing up with this, so use this new superpower wisely.

1 Throw the butternut squash puree and onion in a blender and run until that fucker looks smooth. Set aside.

2 In a small bowl, mix together the flour, cumin, chili powder, and smoked paprika.

3 Grab a medium soup pot and warm the olive oil over medium heat. Throw in the flour mixture and keep stirring until it starts to thicken up and smell kinda toasty. Grab a small whisk and slowly add the vegetable broth while you whisk. It'll start to look like little lumps of Play-Doh. Don't worry, you aren't fucking up. Trust the system. Add the diced tomatoes and their juices and keep stirring; it should be a lot smoother looking now with just some tasty tomato chunks.

4 Now pour in the squash-onion mixture, nooch, garlic, jalapeños, lime juice, and salt. Stir well so there aren't any chunks, and reduce the heat to low. Let everything simmer together for 3 to 5 minutes so the flavors get all mixed up and the sauce thickens. Taste and add whatever you think it needs to get right by you and your crew. Serve up that golden goodness warm and right away.

You can use canned puree, but it's easy as hell to make: Skin and chop up a butternut squash into chunks about the size of a coin until you get about 3 cups. Throw it in a pot with a steamer basket and some water, cover, and steam until the squash is tender, about 15 minutes. Throw it in a blender or food processor and boom, fucking puree.

** Canned is cool here.

*** WTF? See page 231.

HOUSE RULES

Don't waste your cash on some crappy centerpiece you'll never use again. Keep your money and set the mood by saving all those cans you've been using for beans and tomatoes and whatever. Rinse out the empties, peel off the labels, and poke a bunch of holes in the sides with a drill or a hammer and a nail. Drop tea lights inside those motherfuckers and call them constellation cans.

COUNT ON CAULIFLOWER

AND SAY GOODBYE TO SUSPECT SEAFOOD

LANDLOCKED CEVICHE

So yeah, there's no seafood in this dish, but we don't think your ass will miss it, and the fish won't be mad either. Instead we've got the always-affordable cauliflower stepping in. The lime juice breaks down that fibrous motherfucker resulting in a tasty-ass salad or dip that you won't want to share. Just cancel the party now and keep it to yourself.

1 small head of cauliflower, chopped into tiny-ass bites (about 2½ cups)

2 cups diced tomatoes (about 4 medium)

½ cup chopped red onion

1 jalapeño, diced

¼ teaspoon salt

½ cup lime juice

¼ cup chopped cilantro

1 avocado, diced

Black pepper, to taste

1 In a medium bowl, mix together the cauliflower, tomatoes, red onion, jalapeño, salt, and lime juice. Add the cilantro and let that sit in the fridge for at least 1 hour so that the lime juice has some time to soften everything up. That's its job, so let that fucker work.

2 Add the avocado and serve right away, with black pepper to taste.

Keep your salsa, dips, and salads from being a watered-down mess by removing the guts from your tomatoes as you chop. Those seeds and the gel (total technical term) that holds them in place add zero fucking flavor and are only holding your snack game back.

Want to make this shit the night before? Just leave out the cilantro and avocado until right before you serve it so they don't get all gnarly looking while soaking overnight.

PARTY PLAYBOOK
→ ✕✕✕

LAID-BACK
MIDDAY FIESTA

Sometimes you just know it's gonna be one of those hot ass days. You can feel that shit before the sun even comes up. Whip up these dishes before your kitchen gets too caliente so you can spend the rest of your day eating good and sitting in front of a fan. Who knows, maybe the fiesta will turn into a siesta. No judgment.

» **LANDLOCKED CEVICHE**
   (page 49)

» **BUTTERNUT SQUASH QUESO-ISH DIP** (page 46)

» **BREAKFAST TEMPEH AND POTATO TACO BAR** (page 29)

» **MICHELADA** (page 204) or **WATERMELON-STRAWBERRY TEQUILA PUNCH** (page 193)

ROASTED POTATOES
WITH RED PEPPER DIPPING SAUCE

MAKES ENOUGH
FOR 4 PEOPLE,
BUT YOU CAN DOUBLE
OR TRIPLE, NO
FUCKING PROBLEM

The potatoes are just a suggestion because they make an easy party snack, but we swear, the red pepper sauce is dope on almost everything. Spread it on a sandwich, serve it with some raw veggies, put it on toast, your finger, whatever you've got. It will improve some of the dullest parties just by being there. You know, kinda like you.

1 Crank your oven to 425°F. Grab a rimmed baking sheet.

2 In a medium bowl, toss together the potatoes, oil, cornmeal, paprika, and salt until the potatoes are all covered a little bit. Pour them out onto the baking sheet and bake until the potatoes start looking nice and golden brown, 25 to 30 minutes, stirring halfway.

3 While the potatoes are roasting, make the dip: Throw everything together in a blender or small food processor and let that run until it looks kinda smooth. Pour it into a kick-ass-looking glass or bowl and stick it in the fridge. This should make about 1 cup.

4 When the potatoes are done, dump them onto a plate with a bowl of the dipping sauce, sprinkle with the chives, and serve.

* The kind of finely ground cornmeal you'd use to make cornbread, not gritty-ass polenta.

** No fucking clue? See page 217.

*** Need help toasting? See page 218.

1 pound small yellow or red potatoes, sliced in half

2 teaspoons olive oil

1 tablespoon cornmeal*

½ teaspoon smoked paprika

Pinch of salt

¼ cup chopped chives or green onions

RED PEPPER DIPPING SAUCE

2 roasted red bell peppers**

¼ cup sliced almonds, raw or toasted***

2 tablespoons vegetable broth or water

1 tablespoon tomato paste

1 tablespoon sherry vinegar or red wine vinegar

1 clove garlic

2 teaspoons olive oil

½ teaspoon smoked paprika

¼ teaspoon salt

ROASTED BEET HUMMUS

Everybody knows beets are fucking gross all alone. But nobody knows how amazing they can be in a dip with some tahini. Not only is this dip full of iron and protein, it's goddamn gorgeous.

1½ pounds beets,
roasted, peeled,
and chopped*

1½ cups chickpeas**

3 cloves garlic

2 tablespoons tahini***

2 tablespoons olive oil

2 tablespoons lemon
juice

2 tablespoons orange
juice

½ teaspoon salt

**WALNUT-HERB
CRUMBLE**
¼ cup walnuts,
toasted****

3 tablespoons minced
fresh dill

3 tablespoons minced
green onions

Pinch of salt

1 In a food processor or blender, combine the beets, chickpeas, garlic, tahini, olive oil, citrus juices, and salt. Run that shit until everything looks smooth. If it's getting caught up, add a tablespoon of water to help it out. Done.

2 To make the crumble: Just chop up the walnuts all teeny tiny and mix them in a small bowl with the dill, green onions, and salt.

3 Sprinkle the walnut-herb mixture over the dip and serve. The dip is awesome cold or at room temperature and can totally be made a day ahead. Save the crumble for the day of, though, so those herbs stay looking all green and shit.

No clue how to roast a beet? We've got you on page 216.

** A 15-ounce can of chickpeas, drained and rinsed, is a legit choice here.*

*** Tahini is like peanut butter but made out of sesame seeds and equally delicious. It will be near either the peanut butter or the falafel mix at the store.*

**** Need help getting toasted? See page 218.*

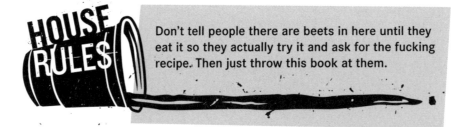

HOUSE RULES

Don't tell people there are beets in here until they eat it so they actually try it and ask for the fucking recipe. Then just throw this book at them.

1 **Roasted Potatoes**
(page 51)

2 **Creamy Pesto Dip**
(page 67)

3 **Roasted Beet Hummus**
(page 52)

4 **Red Pepper Dipping
Sauce** (page 51)

5 **Cork Corpse**

STUFFED MUSHROOMS

MAKES 25, ENOUGH FOR 6 TO 8 PEOPLE, ASSUMING THEY'RE EATING OTHER GRUB, TOO

Stuff the fuck out of these mushrooms, throw on some parsley for looks, and serve immediately with some toothpicks. Your party people won't be able to get enough of these warm little fuckers, but the "fun guy" jokes will never stop no matter how much you beg.

25 large button or cremini mushrooms

2 teaspoons olive oil

½ medium yellow or white onion

½ cup cooked millet or quinoa*

2 cloves garlic, minced

2 green onions, finely chopped (about ¼ cup)

¼ cup chopped fresh dill or parsley

½ teaspoon grated lemon zest**

½ teaspoon salt

¼ teaspoon black pepper

Spray oil

1 Crank your oven to 375°F. Set aside a rimmed baking sheet.

2 First, rip the stems out of the mushrooms so there's someplace to put the filling. Set those fungi fuckers aside while you get the filling ready.

3 In a medium skillet or wok, heat the olive oil over medium heat. Add the onion and sauté it around until it starts to look a little golden, about 5 minutes. Add the millet, garlic, and green onions and cook that all together for another minute until the green onion starts looking less raw. Fold in the dill, lemon zest, salt, and pepper and remove from the heat. Taste here and add more shit if you think more garlic or herbs are what you'd like.

4 Now it's time to stuff. Transfer the filling to a bowl and let it cool down for a few. Grab your mushrooms and fill each mushroom up, like domed up full, with a spoonful of the filling and place them on the baking sheet, filling side up, obvs. Keep going until you run out of 'shrooms. Spray the tops with a little oil and bake those fuckers up until the tops start looking nice and crispy, 15 to 20 minutes.

5 Serve warm because cold, cooked whole mushrooms can be chewy as hell.

* No clue how to do that shit? See page 213.

** Need help zesting? See page 218.

DON'T LET TAKEOUT
TAKE YOU FOR A RIDE

BAKED SPRING ROLLS

Frying food at home can be the worst; it stinks up your place and you inevitably burn the fuck outta yourself. But don't get lazy and grab the takeout menu. Roll yourself up some of these crispy sons of bitches and get all the taste without any of the bullshit.

MAKES ABOUT 12 ROLLS, DEPENDING ON THE SIZE OF THE WRAPPERS YOU GRAB

2 teaspoons neutral oil, such as grapeseed

1 cup sliced shiitake or button mushrooms

1 carrot, cut into thin matchsticks

1 large rib celery, cut into thin matchsticks

1 head of napa or green cabbage, cut into bite-size strips (about 4½ cups)

¼ cup minced green onions

1 cup cooked glass noodles*

1½ tablespoons soy sauce or tamari

1 tablespoon rice vinegar

¼ teaspoon black pepper

12 large spring roll wrappers

Spray oil

DIPPING SAUCE (OPTIONAL)
1 tablespoon soy sauce or tamari

1 tablespoon rice vinegar

1 tablespoon water

1 teaspoon Asian-style hot sauce

1 teaspoon toasted sesame oil

1 teaspoon agave syrup

1 clove garlic, minced

* WTF? See page 214.

1 Crank your oven to 400°F. Grab a large rimmed baking sheet.

2 In a large wok or skillet, warm up the oil over medium-high heat. Throw in the mushrooms, carrot, and celery and sauté until the mushrooms start to release a little of their liquid, about 2 minutes. Add the cabbage and green onions and cook until the cabbage has started to really cook down, about 3 minutes longer. It should now look like a normal amount of cabbage and not a shit-ton of leaves. Add the noodles, soy sauce or tamari, vinegar, and pepper and mix it around until there aren't a bunch of dry-ass noodle or cabbage pockets hiding out. Remove from the heat.

3 To make the spring rolls, lay out one of the wrappers so one of the corners is pointed right at your body. Keep the remaining wrappers covered with a moist cloth or paper towel because they dry out really fucking quick. Turn the page to follow along.

Fig. 1: Grab a forkful of the filling and throw it down on the bottom third of the wrapper closest to you. Use some water on your fingers to get the edges all wet. This will help these fuckers close up in a second.

(continued)

| Fig. 1 | Fig. 2 | Fig. 3 |

Fig. 2: Fold the bottom point of the wrapper up over the pile of filling, roll it once, then fold in the two side points so this shit looks like a child's drawing of a 2 story house.

Fig. 3: Keep rolling until it's all tight. Spray it gently with a bit of oil and place that deliciousness seam-side down on the baking sheet.

4 Keep going until you run out of filling or wrappers but you should get at least 12 outta all that shit. If you're worried about how much filling you are piling in, always do a little less than you think. The more wrapper there is vs. the filling the crispier these little flavor cigars will be.

5 Throw the baking sheet in the oven and bake, turning the rolls halfway through, until both sides are golden and crispy, 30 to 35 minutes.

6 You can mix up the optional dipping sauce while the spring rolls are baking by just throwing the soy sauce or tamari, rice vinegar, water, hot sauce, sesame oil, agave, and garlic in a small bowl and stirring. Fucking done.

7 Let the rolls cool for a couple minutes and then serve those golden brown bitches with some dipping sauce and watch people lose their goddamn minds when they find out it's not takeout.

PAN-ROASTED PEPPERS

SERVES ABOUT
4 PEOPLE WHO JUST
CAME TO SNACK

Padrón and shishito peppers look a ton alike and are cheap as hell come spring and summer. With both of them, only one in every ten is actually hot, so it's kinda like playing Russian roulette with your taste buds. Warning: The hot one will find its way to the person least able to handle their shit. It's like science or something.

2 tablespoons olive oil

1 pound Padrón or shishito peppers

Squeeze of lemon juice

Pinch of salt

1 Grab a large wok or skillet and heat up 1 tablespoon of the oil over high heat. Throw in half the peppers and stir them around every now and then. Keep cooking until the skins on the peppers look black in some places and they are starting to soften, about 5 minutes. Throw them in a medium bowl and repeat with the remaining peppers and oil.

2 When all the peppers are done, squeeze in a little lemon juice, mix, sprinkle in the salt, and toss again. Serve right away with some drinks handy.

HOUSE RULES

Want to mix up the flavors? Replace the salt with a splash of soy sauce or tamari and ¼ teaspoon toasted sesame oil and you've got a whole new fucking dish. ACHIEVEMENT UNLOCKED: SUPER SIMPLE BONUS RECIPE

**MAKES 1 BIG-ASS
FUCKING LOAF
OF BREAD**

2 teaspoons plus
2 tablespoons olive oil

1 medium yellow onion,
sliced into thin strips

1 large apple, halved,
cored, and sliced into
thin half-moons*

1 teaspoon lemon juice

1 tablespoon chopped
fresh thyme or rosemary

Everyday Pizza Dough
(page 226)

1 tablespoon
unsweetened nondairy
milk of your choice

**BALSAMIC DIPPING
SAUCE (OPTIONAL)**
3 tablespoons balsamic
vinegar

3 tablespoons olive oil

1 small clove garlic,
minced

2 tablespoons minced
fresh parsley

Pinch of red pepper
flakes

*Granny Smith, Pink Lady,
whateverthefuck you're
willing to eat will work here.*

APPLE-ONION FOCACCIA

This motherfucker will make your whole place smell like fall even in the middle of spring. And yeah, that's a damn good thing.

___

1 Crank your oven up to 450°F. Grease a rimmed baking sheet so your bread doesn't stick.

2 In a medium skillet, heat up 1 teaspoon of the olive oil over medium heat. Add the onion and sauté those fuckers around until they look kinda brown and delicious, 5 to 7 minutes. Scrape the onion out of the pan onto a plate.

3 Throw another 1 teaspoon olive oil into the same pan. Add the apple slices and cook them over medium heat. Add the lemon juice and thyme and sauté until the apple slices are slightly browned, 5 to 7 minutes total. Remove from the heat, cuz it's dough time.

4 On a well-floured surface, shape your dough into a 4 x 10-inch rectangle about an inch or so thick. Don't pull out a fucking ruler, just eyeball that shit. Place that on your super greased-up baking sheet. Take your fingertips and dimple the top of the bread like you're a phantom of the opera, or some shit like that, playing the organ in a dramatic way. You know what the fuck we're saying. Mix the remaining 2 tablespoons of olive oil with the milk and brush this all over the dough.

5 Scatter half the onions all over the bread, dimple that shit a little more, and then lay down all the apple slices in a single layer. Make a cool or dumb pattern, spell out *fuck*, whatever. Scatter on the rest of the onions and then throw that shit in the oven. Bake until the bread looks nice and golden, 15 to 25 minutes. Serve warm or at room temp.

6 If you are making the dipping sauce, just mix all the ingredients together on a low-rimmed plate or bowl and get to fucking dipping.

GOTTA BAKE BREAD
TO BREAK IT

CHEX-ISH MIX

With half the fat and waaayyyy less sodium
than the OG version, you can snack away
without feeling like there's a cement mixer
in your gut.

8 cups square, waffle-cut cereal, such as Chex*

1 cup pretzel sticks or circles

1 cup mixed nuts (whatever mix you find is good)

SEASONING MIX

1 tablespoon paprika

1 teaspoon onion powder

1 teaspoon garlic powder

½ teaspoon chili powder

⅛ teaspoon cayenne pepper (optional)**

⅛ teaspoon black pepper

1 tablespoon soy sauce, tamari, or Bragg's***

1 tablespoon sherry vinegar

¼ cup olive oil

1 Warm the oven to 250°F. Pull out 2 rimmed baking sheets and set that shit aside.

2 Grab a big-ass bowl and dump in the cereal, pretzels, and nuts.

3 Make the seasoning mix: In a small glass, mix together the paprika, onion powder, garlic powder, chili powder, cayenne (if using), and black pepper. Whisk in the soy sauce and sherry vinegar so you get a kind of paste. Slowly whisk in the olive oil.

4 Pour the seasoning mix all over the big bowl of cereal and keep mixing until everything looks coated. Pour it out into a single layer on the baking sheets and bake for 1 hour, stirring it up every 15 minutes so it gets evenly toasted.

5 Serve it right away or let it cool down to room temp and store it for your next snack attack. It'll keep for about 2 weeks.

* You can do half rice cereal, half corn, some wheat, whateverthefuck you like or is on sale.

** Optional but fucking awesome. If you know you like heat, go up to ¼ teaspoon for delicious results.

*** WTF? See page 231.

HOUSE RULES

Make this mix your own. Sub in bagel chips for the nuts, add more pretzel, whatever the fuck you like. Just keep the total amount of dry shit to 10 cups so that everything gets enough seasoning and you are good to grub.

BRAISED RADISH BITES

Radishes can be really hit or miss with us, but this recipe is a hit every fucking time. Raw radishes can be bitter as hell but these braised bitches have all the flavor without any of the bite. Even confirmed radish haters like us get down with this shit.

1 bunch of radishes (about 10 globes)

2 teaspoons olive oil

¼ cup thinly sliced shallots or yellow onion

¼ cup water

1 tablespoon balsamic vinegar

Pinch of salt

Parsley, for garnish (optional)

1 Radishes are dirty little fuckers, so make sure to rinse the hell outta them before you get cooking. Trim off the greens from the radishes and slice the globes into halves if they're about the size of Ping-Pong balls and into quarters if they're big as fuck.

2 In a medium skillet, heat the oil over medium heat. Add the shallots and sauté until they start to look brownish, about 5 minutes. Add the radishes to the pan with a cut side facing down. Cook the radishes without touching them for about 5 minutes. I know you wanna fuck with them, but just let them chill. After 5 minutes, add the water, vinegar, and salt.

3 Cover the pan and let the radishes continue to cook until the liquid has evaporated from the pan and the radishes are tender, 8 to 10 minutes. No lid for the pan? Just cover it with some foil. Garnish with some parsley, if you like, and serve up.

DEVILED CHICKPEA BITES

1½ cups cooked chickpeas*

4 teaspoons white wine vinegar

2 tablespoons minced shallot or yellow onion

2 tablespoons olive oil

1 tablespoon water

1 tablespoon nooch**

1¼ teaspoons Dijon mustard

¼ teaspoon salt

½ baguette, cut into slices no thicker than ½ inch

1 large cucumber, thinly sliced***

1 bunch of chives, minced

Paprika

You're not still fucking around with deviled eggs, are you? That app is more antiquated than your grandmother's sweaty Jell-O salad and tastes just as boring. Try these delicious deviled motherfuckers and bring your buffet table into the 21st century.

1 To make the filling, throw the chickpeas, vinegar, shallot, oil, water, nooch, mustard, and salt into a blender or food processor and let that shit run until it looks all creamy. If your machine sucks, add another tablespoon of water to get it going.

2 To assemble the bites, smear a little of the chickpea mix on the bread slices so that the cucumbers stick, then place 2 slices of cucumbers on the bread so that the surface is mostly covered. Now you can just spoon 1½ tablespoons worth of the chickpea mix on the cucumber slices or you can use the lazy pastry bag method from page 229 and pile that shit on like you're out to impress some motherfuckers.

3 Sprinkle the chives over the top and shake on some paprika for looks. Serve within a couple hours of making so that the bread and cucumbers don't get soggy.

* One 15-ounce can of chickpeas, drained and rinsed, is no problem

** WTF? See page 231.

*** You can leave the skin on the cucumber if 1) It isn't too waxy and 2) You're down with that shit. Clearly, we are.

SHIT LOOKS CLASSY AS FUCK

ONE PICNIC
TO RULE THEM ALL

Hungry? Want to get outta the house? Good, you fucking need some fresh air and your couch needs a break. Pack these dishes up and get your ass outside. Find a flat spot with some shade and post up to grub down. Invite some homies but tell them there is a zero-tolerance policy on Hacky Sack and Frisbee golf. ZERO. TOLERANCE.

» **ROASTED BEET HUMMUS** (page 52)

» **CREAMY PESTO DIP** (opposite)

» **PANZANELLA** (page 94) or **FOUR-BEAN SALAD** (page 84)

» **TLTA SAMMIES** (page 138)

» **ROSEMARY CARAMEL CORN** (page 173) or **FRESH CORN BUTTER PIE** (page 184)

EVERYDAY GUACAMOLE

This is for the sad fucks of the world who still have no idea how to make this.

1 In a medium bowl, mash up the avocado to your desired consistency. Mix in the onion, garlic, pepper, lime juice, cumin, and salt.

2 Once that shit is all combined, fold in the cilantro and tomato if you're doing that shit. Taste and add more of whatever the fuck you think, but if you add mayo or sour cream we'll drive over there ourselves and slap the shit out of you for disrespecting guacamole like that. Goddamn.

MAKES ABOUT
1½ CUPS, DEPENDING
ON THE SIZE OF
YOUR AVOCADOS

2 avocados, preferably Hass

¼ cup diced red or white onion

1 clove garlic, minced

1 jalapeño or Fresno pepper, minced

Juice of ½ lime

¼ teaspoon ground cumin

Pinch of salt

3 tablespoons chopped cilantro (optional)*

1 tomato (optional),* chopped

* Both optional as fuck, but delicious.

CREAMY PESTO DIP

Every reason to make this is right in the title.

1 Place the almonds in a food processor or blender and pulse those nutty bitches around until they start getting kinda broken up. Add the basil, garlic, lemon zest, lemon juice, oil, water, and salt, and pulse for another 15 seconds.

2 Add the beans and let that fucker run until it looks nice and smooth. If you're having trouble getting that shit to blend, add another tablespoon of water, nature's lube.

3 Serve right away with some bread or veggies or let it chill in the fridge until cold.

MAKES ABOUT
1 CUP, ENOUGH
FOR 2 TO 4 PEOPLE

¼ cup sliced or slivered almonds

⅓ cup chopped fresh basil

3 cloves garlic, chopped

½ teaspoon grated lemon zest

3 tablespoons lemon juice

2 tablespoons olive oil

2 tablespoons water

¼ teaspoon salt

1½ cups white or cannellini beans*

* A 15-ounce can of beans, drained and rinsed, is legit too.

ROASTED GARLIC PULL-APART BREAD

GARLIC SAUCE
2 bulbs garlic, roasted
(page 217)

1 clove raw garlic

¼ cup olive oil

¼ teaspoon grated lemon zest*

1 tablespoon lemon juice

⅛ teaspoon paprika**

Pinch of salt

BREAD
1 loaf crusty French bread

2 teaspoons nooch***

¼ cup chopped fresh parsley**

This fucker has everything: carbs, garlic.
Literally EVERYTHING.

1 Warm up your oven to 350°F.

2 Make the garlic sauce: Grab your blender or food processor and squeeze all the roasted garlic right out of their skins into the blender. Add the raw garlic, oil, lemon zest, lemon juice, paprika, and salt and run that shit until the mixture looks nice and smooth.

3 Grab your loaf of bread and a sharp, serrated knife. Cut the bread in slices, almost all the way through the loaf, diagonally from corner to corner in both directions (check the photo if we aren't making any fucking sense).

4 Using a knife or pastry brush, smear the garlic sauce inside all the open cuts on the bread. Sprinkle in the nooch, wrap that fucker in foil, and throw it in the oven to get all toasty, about 20 minutes.

5 Sprinkle with the parsley and serve as soon as it's cool enough to eat.

Need help zesting? See page 218.

** *Both paprika and parsley are just for looks. If you don't have them, don't stress.*

*** *WTF? See page 231.*

COME TOGETHER TO
TEAR SHIT APART

SALADS, SAUCES, AND SIDES

LOADED NACHOS

4 to 5 handfuls warm tortilla chips*

1½ cups cooked black beans**

1 cup thinly sliced cabbage or romaine lettuce

Butternut Squash Queso-ish Dip (page 46)

Everyday Guacamole (page 67)

Your favorite chunky-style salsa***

1 jalapeño, sliced into thin circles

¼ cup chopped cilantro

Hot sauce (optional)

OK, this is less of a recipe and more of a recommendation for you to get your shit together and make some fucking nachos. A plate of these gorgeous motherfuckers just screams party so much that it was almost our cover shot. We give you an idea below on how to pile your shit correctly, but take the damn queso and run with it. #nachobusiness

1 You know how nachos work, so you can pile this shit on however you like and leave off or add whatever the fuck you want. We like to put the warm chips out in a thin layer on a tray or giant plate. A huge pile of chips where you end up with a shit-ton of dry chips at the bottom is a fucking bummer. Thin layer is the way to go.

2 Scatter the black beans and cabbage over that, then drizzle the queso all over the chips. Glob on nice spoonfuls of guacamole and salsa all over the platter then sprinkle with the jalapeño and cilantro. Drizzle over some hot sauce if you roll like that.

3 Serve that shit right up to the happy crowd.

* Warming not required, but this shows commitment to the nacho cause. Just throw the chips in a microwave for a few seconds, or cover and put in a 250°F oven for 10 minutes.

** Or a 15-ounce can of beans, rinsed and drained.

*** The Mid-Summer Salsa from our first book would be dope here.

NOT-CHO
AVERAGE
NACHO

TWICE-BAKED POTATOES

Twice-baked potatoes are the kind of nostalgic food that we should never have stopped making. Potatoes stuffed with kale, garlic, onion, and all kinds of deliciousness? Who the fuck wouldn't like that? Serve it alongside a Big-Ass Salad Bowl (page 91) and the Grilled Veggie and Tempeh Kebabs (page 136) and make this a motherfucking meal.

3 large russet (baking) potatoes (about 3 pounds total),* scrubbed but with the skin still on

1 tablespoon olive oil

½ large yellow onion, chopped

3 cups chopped kale or spinach

3 cloves garlic, minced

1½ cups cooked white or navy beans**

⅓ cup unsweetened nondairy milk

2 tablespoons lemon juice

½ teaspoon smoked paprika

½ teaspoon salt

¼ teaspoon black pepper

Spray oil

1 First you got to make some baked potatoes, also known as the first bake. If you are going to do that shit in the oven, crank it up to 400°F. Stab the potatoes all over with a fork so that the steam can escape when you stick the spuds in the oven. Bake until you can stab them with a small knife without any resistance, about 1 hour. If you're using the much-fucking-faster microwave method, stab those sons of bitches all over with a fork just the same. Microwave them on high for 10 to 12 minutes, flipping them halfway. Test by stabbing them with a small knife and keep microwaving until the knife stabs easy. The time will vary based on how beat down your microwave is.

2 While all that shit is going down, start making the filling. Heat a large skillet or wok over medium-high and add the oil. Throw in the onion and stir around until it starts looking really good and brown, 6 to 8 minutes. Add the kale and keep sautéing until it starts to really cook down, like 3 to 5 minutes depending on how hearty that shit is. Fold in the garlic and remove from the heat.

3 In a blender or food processor, combine the beans and milk and run that shit until the beans are all broken down. Set that aside.

4 Now it's time to stuff and twice-bake. Crank that oven back up to 400°F. When the cooked potatoes are cool enough that you can fuck with them, halve them lengthwise and scoop out most of that fluffy white middle into a large bowl. You want to leave about ¼ inch of skin and some potato flesh so that these skins can kinda stand on their own. Yeah, you just read skin and flesh in the same sentence in a plant-based cookbook. Deal with it. Mash the insides of the cooked potato until there are many chunks. Stir in the bean/milk mixture and keep trying to break up any big potato clumps. Fold in the kale and onions, lemon juice, paprika, salt, and black pepper. Taste and add more of whatever the fuck you think it needs.

5 Arrange the potato skins on a rimmed baking sheet. Take big spoonfuls of the filling and pile it in the skins, gently pressing that shit down so that they are all filled up and sorta domed over. Spray the tops with a little oil and bake until the tops are looking golden and kinda toasty, 25 to 35 minutes. Sprinkle some extra paprika on top if you wanna be fancy. Serve warm.

* Yeah, just grab the biggest damn potatoes you can find.

** A 15-ounce can of beans, drained and rinsed, is cool too.

GO BIG OR GO GNOME

PARTY PLAYBOOK
✕✕✕

POTLUCK AT THE PARK

Throwing a potluck at the local park? Fuck yeah, now that's a good time with a low price tag. No need to worry about the menu because with these dishes you've got the potluck on lock. Instead, spend your time worrying about locking down one of the picnic tables away from that big-ass hornet's nest.

POPPY SEED POTATO SALAD

This is a reboot of an old family staple with half the fat but all the flavor. And there's no such thing as having too many potato salad recipes.

MAKES ENOUGH FOR 6 PEOPLE, OR A BIG-ASS BOWL AT A PICNIC

1 Make the dressing: In a blender or food processor, combine the oil, vinegars, shallot, and mustard and run until that onion is fucking invisible. No blender? Just chop that shit up extra tiny. Stir in the poppy seeds and set aside.

2 Make the salad: Chop the potatoes into big, bite-size pieces. If they're really tiny you can just leave them whole. Boil some water in a large pot, add a pinch of salt, and the potatoes. Boil them until you can easily stab a fork through one, like 15 to 25 minutes depending on the size of your potatoes. If you cook them too long they'll start falling apart and your salad will be a damn mess. Set a timer if your ass gets easily distracted. You're already checking Instagram while reading this, aren't you?

3 When the potatoes are tender, drain them and throw them in a large bowl. Add the celery, carrots, and green onions, then pour the dressing all over that bitch. Add the salt and some pepper and mix that motherfucker up so everything is cooked. Let the salad sit in the fridge for at least 30 minutes so that the potatoes can soak in all the flavor. If it looks dry after that, then add a little more vinegar and olive oil to get it going. Serve right away or make this shit the night before the party. Nobody will fucking know and we won't snitch.

* The poppy seeds in this dish make it extra dope, but if you can't find them or don't wanna spend the extra cash, just leave them out. It'll still be legit.

DRESSING
⅓ cup olive oil

¼ cup white wine vinegar

¼ cup rice vinegar

¼ cup chopped shallot or onion

1 tablespoon Dijon mustard

1 tablespoon poppy seeds*

SALAD
2 pounds yellow or red potatoes

Pinch of salt

4 ribs celery, chopped (about 1 cup)

2 medium carrots, shredded (about 1 cup)

⅓ cup finely chopped green onions

¼ teaspoon salt

Black pepper to taste

COLD NOODLE AND HERB SALAD

This dish is perfect for when it's hot as a motherfucker outside and a straight lettuce salad just won't cut it. Throw in some baked tofu from our first book and turn this shit into an entrée for your dinner party or picnic.

SCALLION DRESSING

½ cup chopped green onions*

2 cloves garlic, chopped

⅓ cup rice vinegar

3 tablespoons toasted sesame oil

1 tablespoon lemon or lime juice

2 teaspoons Sriracha-style hot sauce

1 teaspoon agave syrup or your favorite liquid sweetener

SALAD

1 pound thin noodles, cooked**

2 carrots, cut into matchsticks

1 red bell pepper, cut into matchsticks

½ medium cucumber, cut into matchsticks

1½ cups shelled edamame***

½ cup chopped fresh basil

½ cup chopped cilantro

2 tablespoons toasted sesame seeds (optional)****

1 First make the dressing: Throw the green onions, garlic, vinegar, sesame oil, lemon juice, Sriracha, and agave into a blender or food processor and let that shit run until everything looks mixed up and the green onions are in little bits. You don't fucking need it to be silky smooth, so don't go fucking crazy. Like 15 to 30 seconds max. Then just set aside. Or you can mince up the green onions and garlic by hand and mix all the shit together in a jar. Whatever you're about.

2 Put the salad together: In a large bowl, combine the noodles, carrots, bell pepper, cucumber, and edamame. Pour in the dressing and mix until everything looks coated and all the veggies are mingling with the noodles. Fold in the basil, cilantro, and sesame seeds (if using). Cover and set it in the fridge to chill for at least an hour before serving.

Scallions and green onions are the same damn thing. We just called them "scallions" in the name of the dressing cause it sounds badass, but now you know the truth.

** *Soba, udon, or regular ol' spaghetti would work just fine here. Use what you've got. See page 213 for a pasta breakdown.*

*** *See House Rules on page 6.*

**** *Optional, but sesame seeds kinda class up the dish. People love tiny-ass seeds; details like that makes them feel like their food is special. Not a deal breaker if you don't have them though. Need help toasting? See page 218.*

ITALIAN-STYLE PASTA SALAD

MAKES ENOUGH FOR
4 TO 6 PEOPLE

Stop buying some corn syrup—laced bottled dressing to make your pasta salad. That shit tastes subpar and you aren't fooling anybody saying that the salad is homemade. You didn't cook shit, you just assembled it. That's like putting together Ikea furniture and calling yourself a carpenter.

Italian Dressing (recipe follows on page 82)

1 pound pasta*

1 small crown of broccoli, chopped into bite-size pieces (about 2 cups)

1 red bell pepper, roasted or raw, chopped (about 1 cup)**

1 cup chopped cucumber (about ½ cucumber)

1 pint cherry or grape tomatoes, halved

½ cup sliced red onion (about ½ small)

⅓ cup chopped fresh basil

¼ cup sliced black olives (optional)**

½ teaspoon salt

Black pepper to taste

1 Make the dressing and set aside.

2 Cook the pasta according to the package directions. While the pasta is boiling away, cut up all your veggies. About 30 seconds before the pasta is done, add the broccoli. This will soften it up a little for the salad because we're too lazy to steam that shit separately. You, too? Awesome. Drain the whole thing and run under cool water to stop that broccoli from overcooking.

3 Grab a big-ass bowl and throw in the cooked pasta and broccoli, the bell pepper, cucumber, tomatoes, red onion, basil, and olives (if using). Pour the dressing on top and toss that shit together. Add the salt and a little pepper and keep tossing. Stick it in the fridge and let it chill out for at least an hour because there's no such thing as hot pasta salad, that's just pasta. Practice some damn patience. Taste and then add whatthefuckever else it might need.

4 Serve cool or at room temperature.

* We like rotini but you can use penne, big macaroni, or large shells. Whatever you like is cool. No angel hair though, you goddamn amateur.

** Don't know how to roast a damn pepper? See page 217.

*** Optional, but people will be expecting that olive shit.

(continued)

ITALIAN DRESSING

MAKES ABOUT 1 CUP

⅓ cup olive oil
½ cup white wine vinegar
2 tablespoons lemon juice
2 cloves garlic, minced
¾ teaspoon dried basil
¾ teaspoon dried thyme
¾ teaspoon onion powder
Black pepper to taste

In a small jar, combine the oil, vinegar, lemon juice, garlic, dried basil, thyme, onion powder, and pepper and mix that shit up.

1 **Four-Bean Salad**
(page 84)

2 **Italian-Style Pasta Salad** (page 81)

3 **High School-Style Hard Lemonade** (page 198)

4 **Old-School Radio**

FOUR-BEAN SALAD

This picnic staple is always grabbed last minute at the store and usually full of some sad, soggy-ass beans. Stop insulting your friends and family with that store-bought sadness and just make this shit yourself. Find out how goddamn delicious this is meant to be after all those years of subpar salads. Plus you'll get a ton of the protein that we know people are always asking you about.

DRESSING

½ teaspoon Dijon mustard

½ teaspoon your favorite liquid sweetener (like agave syrup)

1 clove garlic, minced

2 tablespoons lemon juice

2 tablespoons rice vinegar

3 tablespoons apple cider vinegar

¼ cup olive oil

SALAD

½ pound green beans,* cut into 1-inch pieces

1½ cups each cooked chickpeas, kidney beans, and cannellini beans**

1¼ cups chopped celery***

½ medium red onion, cut into 1-inch pieces

½ cup chopped fresh parsley****

½ teaspoon garlic powder

½ teaspoon celery seed*****

¼ teaspoon salt

Black pepper to taste

1 Make the dressing: Throw the mustard, sweetener, garlic, lemon juice, vinegars, and olive oil together in a small jar and shake the fuck out of it. Set it aside.

2 Get the salad going: Place a steamer insert and a couple inches of water in a small pot. Bring to a boil over medium heat. Add the green beans, cover, and steam until they're tender but not sad and mushy, 8 to 10 minutes.

3 When the green beans are ready, run them under cold water to chill them out and then dump them into a large bowl with the chickpeas, kidney beans, and cannellini beans. Add the celery, onion, parsley, and the dressing and mix those bean brothers up until everything looks nice and coated. Add the garlic powder, celery seed, salt, and a little pepper. Mix again until everything is distributed.

4 Cover the salad and stick it in the fridge for at least an hour or as long as overnight. Before serving, taste it and see if it needs more salt or pepper, then dig in.

* You could use frozen here instead of fresh, but we aren't down with canned green beans. They are always way too fucking mushy.

** One 15-ounce can of each bean, drained and rinsed, would do too. Also, feel free to mix things up. You could do shelled edamame, navy, and kidney, or whateverthefuck you've got. Just try to mix up colors and the textures so this isn't boring as fuck to eat. All mushy beans = a terrible salad.

*** About 5 ribs celery.

**** We used flat-leaf parsley because we're fancy like that, but use whatever your store stocks.

***** Celery seed is your secret weapon to make food that screams "summer party picnic table shit." It should be with the rest of the spices at the store. If you can't find it, just leave it out and tell your grocery store to get their shit in order.

BE BOUGIE
EAT THISTLES

GRILLED ARTICHOKES WITH ROASTED GARLIC DIP

MAKES ENOUGH
FOR 4 PEOPLE

Make this during peak artichoke season in the spring when the price drops like crazy and you can get that shit for next to nothing. People will think you're superfancy, but we won't tell them the whole spread cost $5.

2 lemons

Salt

4 cloves garlic,
2 smashed and 2 minced

2 large artichokes

¼ cup olive oil

Roasted Garlic Dip
(page 88)

1 Fill a large pot with water and put it over high heat. Squeeze the juice of ½ lemon into the pot and slice up the other half and add it to the water with a good pinch of salt and the 2 cloves of smashed garlic. While that comes to a boil, prep your shit.

2 We know artichokes look alien as fuck, but they're really easy to clean up. Remove all the tough outer leaves around the base and cut 1½ inches off the top of each artichoke. Using a pair of scissors, cut the top off any leaves that still have the barb on them. Disarm that motherfucker. If your artichokes still have their stalks, peel the outside with a vegetable peeler to get at the softer center (see artichoke 1).

3 Halve the artichokes lengthwise. With a spoon, scoop out all the hairy guts, but don't take out the tasty-as-fuck heart (see artichoke 2). By now your pot should be boiling. Add the artichokes and simmer until one of the inside leaves can be pulled out without too much of a fight, 15 to 20 minutes. Let them drain over the sink for a few while you get the grill going.

(continued)

4 Warm up the grill to medium-high. In a bowl, mix together the minced garlic, oil, a pinch of salt, and 2 tablespoons of juice from that last lemon. When the grill is ready to go, brush some of that oil mixture all over the drained chokes.

5 Throw those thistly bastards on the grill, cut side down, and cook until they get some good grill marks on them but the leaves aren't burnt to shit, 2 to 3 minutes. Flip them over and do the same on the other side. Brush with more of the oil mix if you think it needs it.

6 Serve hot or at room temperature with some garlic dip and a big-ass bowl for everyone to throw away their leaves. Eating an artichoke is messy but well worth the trouble.

ROASTED GARLIC DIP

MAKE 1½ CUPS, ENOUGH FOR 6 TO 8 PEOPLE

This is a lot like the Low-Fat Farmhouse Dip on page 45 but garlic-ier. You'll have trouble keeping this shit around for any get-together because someone will eventually just start fucking drinking it straight.

12 ounces soft silken tofu*

5 cloves roasted garlic**

2 tablespoons minced shallot or white onion

1 tablespoon apple cider vinegar or lemon juice

1 tablespoon minced chives

1 tablespoon minced fresh parsley

½ teaspoon salt

1 Throw the tofu, garlic, and shallot into a blender or food processor and run until it looks all smooth. If you put the papery garlic skin in there too, we swear we're going drive over there and confiscate your whole fucking kitchen from you. Damn. Throw in the rest of the ingredients and pulse it a couple of times so everything gets chopped up and mixed in but the herbs are still kinda visible.

2 Let it sit in the fridge at least 1 hour before serving so that the flavors can get to know each other. Serve with whatever vegetables you like and get to dipping. It will keep for 3 or 4 days in the fridge.

Scared of tofu? See page 231.

**Need some help? See page 217.*

ZUCCHINI ROLLUPS

This is basically a raw veggie platter that wishes it was sushi. The rollups might sound healthy/boring as all hell, but you should watch these fuckers disappear off a tray.

MAKES ABOUT 18 TO 24, DEPENDING ON THE SIZE OF YOUR ZUCCHINI

3 medium zucchini

Creamy Pesto Dip (page 67)

2 carrots, cut into 2-inch matchsticks

1 cucumber, cut into 2-inch matchsticks

1 red bell pepper, cut into 2-inch matchsticks

2 green onions, cut into thin strips, or a handful of chives

1 Chop the ends off of your zucchini so they are about the same length. Use a wide vegetable peeler or a sharp knife to cut wide planks of the zucchini lengthwise. Think lasagna noodle for the shape and the thickness, but a little thinner is cool, too. You should get 7 or 8 from each, depending on the zucchini.

2 Now to assemble those motherfuckers. Lay a plank of zucchini down with a short end toward you. Add 1 tablespoon of the pesto dip to the one-third of the plank closest to you. Add a few matchsticks of the veggies and the onions on top of your dip, perpendicular to the plank, keeping them even with one side of the zucchini and letting all the extra hang out on the other damn side. Roll it up away from you and stick a toothpick through it to hold it together and make a nice handle for people to grab the fucker with. Keep going until you run out of dip, zucchini, or goddamn patience.

3 Serve them right away or let them chill in the fridge, covered, for up to 2 hours before serving.

BIG-ASS SALAD BOWL

We know, the last thing you want to bring to a party is a lettuce salad, but this shit is easy to throw together and goes great alongside whatever everyone else brought. Making a salad isn't fucking rocket science but we thought reminding you how to do this shit wasn't a bad idea. You can switch out anything you don't like and use whatever veggies you've got on hand because this fucker is laid-back like that. Just make sure you've got a good mix of crunchy and soft veggies to make the salad interesting.

10 cups mixed greens*

1 cucumber, cut into thin rounds

2 ribs celery, chopped

2 medium tomatoes, chopped

2 carrots, shaved into thin strips with your veggie peeler

1 avocado, sliced or chopped

½ medium red onion, sliced into thin strips

2 small beets, roasted** and cut into cubes or matchsticks

¼ cup chopped fresh herbs, such as chives, dill, cilantro, basil, or a mix of whatever goes with your dressing

1½ cups cooked beans, such as garbanzo, kidney, or black beans

Whatever dressing you are feeling***

Salt and black pepper to taste

So obviously you can just throw this shit all together in a bowl, with the greens on the bottom and dress it when people are ready to eat, but you should take some time with the presentation. We think the best-looking salads are when everything is all grouped together before getting mixed in because it 1. Looks healthy as fuck and 2. Is so pretty that you almost don't want to eat it. So take the time to arrange it up right, like in the photo, and you'll make some friends with salad. Trust.

* Red, greenleaf, butter, romaine, whateverthefuck you like.

** Roasting beets? See page 216.

*** You can dress your salad with whatever the fuck you want—from our Low-Fat Farmhouse Dip made into a dressing (page 45), to our Italian Dressing (page 82), to one of the delicious bastards on page 106. No matter what you pick, people will be embarrassed to ask for the recipe because they can't believe how much they love your shit.

SATURDAY
SLEEPOVER SHIT

No matter how old you are, sometimes you just gotta get in your pjs, build a pillow fort, and have a motherfucking movie marathon. Prep all this the day or morning before, then post out in your dope-ass fort while you nosh on some nutritious shit. Tomorrow you can regret your terrible movie selection and not your food. #Godfather3

QUICK HOMEMADE BBQ SAUCE

Why are you still buying bottled BBQ sauce like some simple son of a bitch? You're better than that syrupy shit. This sauce comes together in a sec and will leave you wondering why the fuck you ever bought an $8 bottle that you used up in one meal. You know what to put this on, but it is particularly badass on the BBQ Bean Sliders (page 127).

1½ cups tomato sauce

¼ cup apple cider vinegar

3 tablespoons brown sugar

2 tablespoons blackstrap molasses*

1 teaspoon Dijon mustard

½ teaspoon liquid smoke**

¼ teaspoon salt

In a small saucepan, mix everything together and bring that shit to a simmer over medium heat. Reduce to low heat and simmer for about 10 minutes, stirring every couple minutes, until it thickens up a little. Serve warm right away or keep it in the fridge for about a week. Pour it on everything. YES. EVERYTHING.

You can use blackstrap or regular molasses. See below.

** *Don't know what this shit is? See page 231.*

HOUSE RULES

Blackstrap has way more fucking iron but is also more bitter than the regular stuff. We use blackstrap, but you do you. Either way, this shit will be near the maple syrup at the store.

PANZANELLA

This is our take on the famous Italian bread salad. Never had that shit before? It's basically the vegetable-to-crouton ratio you've always wanted in a salad but were too ashamed to ask for.

DRESSING

¼ cup red wine vinegar

2 tablespoons lemon juice

2 cloves garlic, minced

¼ cup olive oil

SALAD

½ loaf stale crusty bread,* cut into bite-size cubes (about 6 cups)

1 cup cooked quinoa**

½ small red onion, sliced

2 cups halved cherry or grape tomatoes

1½ cups bite-size pieces of cucumber

1 red bell pepper, chopped

½ cup packed sliced fresh basil

1 cup chopped fresh parsley

¼ teaspoon salt

Black pepper to taste

1 Make the dressing: In a small glass, mix together the vinegar, lemon juice, garlic, and oil until it looks all fucking nice and uniform. Set it aside.

2 Make the salad: In a big bowl, mix together the bread, quinoa, onion, tomatoes, cucumber, and bell pepper. Pour the dressing over the whole salad and mix that shit around. Add the basil, parsley, salt, and pepper to taste and keep mixing until everything is coated. Taste and add more of whateverthefuck you think it needs.

3 Serve right away or let that fucker chill in the fridge for a while. Best served the day it's made 'cause those croutons have a shelf life once they start disintegrating in all the delicious dressing.

* You could use French bread or whatever you got. Sourdough would be our weapon of choice though.

** Reference that shit on page 213.

DOUBLE DOWN ON
DELICIOUSNESS

CALIFORNIA CITRUS AND ALMOND SALAD

MAKES 1 BIG-ASS SALAD, MORE THAN ENOUGH FOR 4 TO 6 PEOPLE

Whoever the fuck thinks you shouldn't serve salads at parties never met this gorgeous green monster. It looks legit and tastes so good that even confirmed salad haters will go for seconds.

1 Make the dressing: Throw everything together in a tiny-ass cup and mix it up with a fork. Stick that shit in the fridge until it's go-time.

2 Make the salad: Put the kale in a large bowl and sprinkle it with the salt. Now get in there with your hands and kinda massage that shit around for about a minute. The salt will help break down the kale a little so the fibrous motherfucker isn't so tough to chew.

3 Add the romaine, green onions, and cilantro. Drizzle in the dressing and toss until everything looks all coated and shiny as shit. Fold in the orange slices and almonds and then taste. Add more vinegar, cilantro, almonds, whateverthefuck you think it needs, then serve right away.

* Need help getting toasted? See page 218.

DRESSING
3 tablespoons rice vinegar

2 tablespoons toasted sesame oil

2 teaspoons minced fresh ginger

1 teaspoon agave syrup or your favorite liquid sweetener

SALAD
1 bunch of kale, tough ribs removed, cut into strips (about 4 cups)

½ teaspoon salt

1 small head of romaine, cut into strips (about 4 cups)

¾ cup sliced green onions (about 3 of those guys)

¼ cup chopped cilantro

2 cups orange segments (about 2 oranges)

1 cup sliced or slivered almonds, toasted*

CURRY TEMPEH SALAD

Put this out as is, serve over some spinach, or do some kickass open-faced sammies by scooping it over toasted bread. Either way, it's a winner.

DRESSING

½ cup plain nondairy yogurt*

1 tablespoon lime or lemon juice

1 tablespoon rice vinegar

2 cloves garlic, minced

2 teaspoons no-salt-added yellow curry powder

½ teaspoon Sriracha-style hot sauce

¼ teaspoon salt

SALAD

8 ounces tempeh,** cut into bite-size pieces

1 teaspoon soy sauce or tamari

1½ cups cooked quinoa***

1 crisp apple, chopped into bite-size pieces

4 ribs celery, chopped

½ cup shredded carrot (about 1 large)

½ cup chopped toasted walnuts****

⅓ cup chopped cilantro

1 Make the dressing: In a medium glass, mix together the yogurt, lime juice, and vinegar until everything is evenly distributed. Throw in the garlic, curry powder, hot sauce, and salt and keep stirring until everything is nice and yellow and there aren't any secret clumps of curry powder or hot sauce hiding around in there. Set that shit in the fridge.

2 Now get your tempeh on: Place a steamer insert and a couple inches of water in a small pot. Bring to a boil over medium heat. Add the tempeh, cover, and steam until it starts to smell kinda nutty, about 10 minutes. Dump it into a large bowl, sprinkle with the soy sauce or tamari, and stir so it gets kinda mixed up. Let it cool while you chop up your veggies.

3 Add the quinoa, apple, celery, carrot, and walnuts to the bowl with the tempeh and mix it all together. Add all of the dressing and the cilantro and keep mixing until everything is coated and looking on point. Taste and add more hot sauce, lime juice, salt, whatever you think might take it up to your level for flavor.

4 Serve right away or let it chill in the fridge until cold, about an hour.

* This is 6 ounces of yogurt or one little plastic cup thing at the store. We used plain coconut yogurt, but use whatever kind your store stocks.

** WTF? See page 231.

*** About ¾ cup uncooked quinoa. No fucking idea beyond that? See page 213.

**** If you hate walnuts, just sub in what kind of nuts you like or keep in the back of your freezer. Pecans, cashews, and almonds would all be legit. Need help getting toasted? See page 218.

YOU DESERVE A LUNCH
THAT WORKS AS HARD
AS YOU PRETEND TO

BLACK BEAN AND CORN SALAD

2 medium red or orange
bell peppers

½ red onion

2 teaspoons olive oil

2 cloves garlic, minced

1 teaspoon chili powder

¼ teaspoon ground
cumin

¼ teaspoon salt

3 cups cooked black
beans*

2 cups corn kernels**

1 jalapeño, seeded and
minced (optional)

⅓ cup chopped cilantro

3 tablespoons lime juice

This simple salad is way more exciting
than the sum of its parts. We know once
you try it, you'll add this fiber-filled
motherfucker to your rotation. If you want
to make this extra fancy, throw in some
avocado chunks and an extra squeeze of
lime. But don't fucking waste your avocado
resources on a crowd if they can't
appreciate nice things.

1 Chop the bell peppers and onion up until they are about the
size of beans. Yeah, you read that shit right: bean-size. Grab a
medium skillet or wok and heat up the oil over medium heat. Add
the onion and cook for 2 minutes to soften up. Add the bell
peppers and cook for a minute more. We're just trying to take the
rawness off those fuckers and make them a little sweeter. Add
the garlic, chili powder, cumin, and salt and cook for an additional
30 seconds, then remove from the heat.

2 Dump the cooked onion/pepper mixture into a large bowl and
add the black beans and corn. (If you're using frozen corn you can
just pour those bastards in cold to speed up the chilling process.)
Add the jalapeño (if using), cilantro, and lime juice and stir that
shit up until it is all mixed. Let it chill on the counter or in the
fridge for 30 minutes and then taste. Add more salt, lime juice, or
garlic to get it where you're satisfied with your salad.

3 Serve chilled or at room temperature as a salad or a dip.

* Two 15-ounces cans of beans are cool. Just drain and rinse that shit.

** Fresh corn kernels cut right off the cob are legit, but you can use whatever you
want. Leftover boiled corn, grilled corn, or frozen all work and are all fucking
awesome. Do what's easiest for you, depending on the time of year you're
whipping this up.

ROASTED WINTER SQUASH WITH MINT

MAKES ENOUGH FOR
6 TO 8 PEOPLE AS
A SIDE

This simple side is perfect to bring for Thanksgiving because it looks much fancier than it is. Go ahead and pretend like you've got your shit together with this and maybe the family will quit asking when you're gonna get married.

2 tablespoons olive oil

½ teaspoon ground cumin

½ teaspoon salt

½ yellow onion, cut into thin strips

2 pounds winter squash,* seeded and cut into 1-inch-thick wedges or rings, but with the skin on for looks

DRESSING

2 tablespoons lemon juice

1 green onion, finely chopped (about 2 tablespoons)

1 tablespoon finely chopped fresh mint

1 clove garlic, minced

Black pepper to taste

1 Crank up your oven to 425°F. Grab 2 rimmed baking sheets. Yeah, sorry, this shit takes 2 of them.

2 In a large bowl, mix together the oil, cumin, and salt. Add the onion and squash and stir that shit around, using your hands or a big-ass spoon until everything has a little something on it. Pour that out in a mostly even layer over the 2 baking sheets and stick them in the oven. Roast, flipping the wedges over halfway, until both sides are nice and golden or browned in some spots, about 30 minutes.

3 While that is roasting, make the dressing: Mix everything together in a small glass.

4 When the squash is all done, dump it all out onto a platter, drizzle the dressing over it, and serve hot. Sprinkle with some pepper and more salt if you think it needs that shit.

* Kabocha, acorn, or delicata squash all are legit as fuck here. You can do one giant squash or two smaller 1-pound guys and mix shit up. As long as you cut them up into the same size, those fuckers will roast at the same rate. And use a sharp knife or you will fucking cut yourself trying to wiggle that shit through. Be careful and have some goddamn sense.

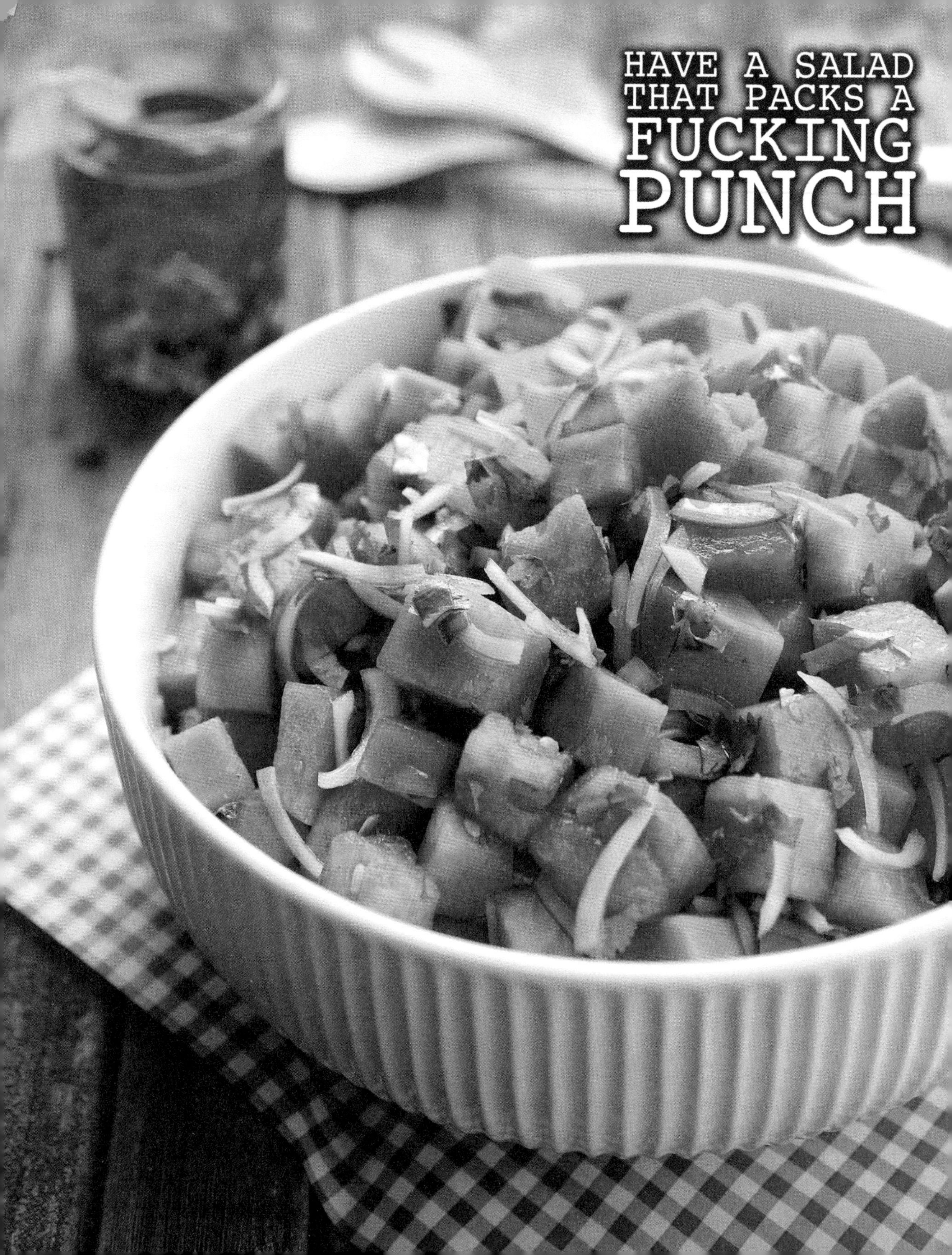
HAVE A SALAD
THAT PACKS A
FUCKING
PUNCH

BOOZY WATERMELON AND PAPAYA SALAD

This is the fruit salad you make when you're feeling grown as fuck. The watermelon and tequila let everyone know that you're here for a good time but the papaya and savory shit tell everyone that you've got classy-as-hell tastes. Go ahead, show them what the fuck you're about.

DRESSING

2 tablespoons lime juice

2 tablespoons tequila

1 tablespoon rice vinegar

2 teaspoons olive oil

2 teaspoons of your favorite liquid sweetener (like agave syrup)

SALAD

1 small watermelon (about 3 pounds), chopped into quarter-size cubes (about 5 cups)

1 small Maradol papaya* (about 2 pounds), chopped into quarter-size cubes (about 4 cups)

½ red onion, thinly sliced

1 jalapeño (optional), seeded and diced**

¼ cup chopped cilantro

¼ teaspoon salt

1 First make the dressing: In a small glass, mix together the lime juice, tequila, vinegar, oil, and agave.

2 Now the salad: In a large bowl, gently mix together the watermelon, papaya, red onion, and jalapeño (if using). You can't be rough with this shit or it will fall apart.

3 Pour the dressing over the whole bowl and fold in the cilantro and salt as you stir that all up. Serve that shit right away.

Papaya, like cilantro, is a love it or hate it kinda deal. If you hate it or can't find it where you're at, just replace it with more watermelon.

**Optional, but if you've come this far, just fucking go for it.*

HOUSE RULES

If you want to make part of this shit ahead of time, just wait until right before you serve the salad to dress it and add the cilantro and salt. The dressing and the salt break down the fruit so it won't look legit if you have it sitting around all made for 6 hours.

COBB SALAD

Yeah, maybe our take on this classic has a couple extra steps more than your average salad, but do you see how fucking beautiful it is? Stop whining and make all the toppings, because those flavor grenades make it worth the trouble.

---

1 First, make the dressing. In a small glass, mix together the mustard, maple syrup, and garlic. Whisk in the vinegars. Then slowly add the oil and stir that shit up until it's all combined. Set it in the fridge until it's go-time.

2 Next, make the onions: In a medium skillet, heat the oil up over medium-high heat. Add the onions and sauté until they start to brown up and look kinda caramelized, 8 to 10 minutes. While that is going down, mix together the soy sauce or tamari, water, and liquid smoke in a small glass. When the onions are done caramelizing, pour the soy sauce mixture over those tasty sons of bitches and cook until all the liquid has evaporated, about 1 minute longer. Scrape them onto a plate and set aside.

3 Now, make the chickpeas: In a small glass, mix together the broth, miso, and soy sauce or tamari. Heat the same skillet the onions were in over medium-high heat and add the oil. Add the chickpeas and cook until they warm up and start to look a little golden in some spots, about 2 minutes. Add the miso sauce and cook until all the liquid has evaporated, 3 to 4 minutes longer. Remove from the heat and stir in the nooch and garlic powder until all the chickpeas are coated.

4 To assemble this super salad: Grab a big-ass platter and cover it in chopped lettuce. Gently pour over some of the dressing with some salt and pepper and toss. Add the avocado, tomatoes, chives, smoky onions, and chickpeas on top in nice little rows so everyone will recognize your sick style. Serve right away.

DRESSING
1 teaspoon yellow mustard

1 teaspoon maple syrup or agave syrup

1 or 2 cloves garlic, minced*

⅓ cup red wine vinegar

1 tablespoon rice vinegar

⅓ cup olive oil

SMOKY ONIONS
1 teaspoon olive oil

½ large yellow onion, sliced

1 teaspoon soy sauce or tamari

1 teaspoon water

1 teaspoon liquid smoke**

MISO-GLAZED CHICKPEAS
2 tablespoons vegetable broth or water

2 teaspoons red miso paste***

½ teaspoon soy sauce or tamari

2 teaspoons olive oil

1½ cups cooked chickpeas****

2 teaspoons nooch**

¼ teaspoon garlic powder

SALAD
1 romaine heart, chopped

1 head of red leaf lettuce, chopped

Salt and black pepper

1 avocado, chopped

2 fist-size tomatoes, chopped

½ cup chopped chives

* You know what you're about. Add the extra garlic.

** WTF? See page 231.

** WTF? See page 231.

*** Really, any miso paste is cool here. Red is just our favorite. Can't find that shit at all? Replace it with 1 teaspoon soy sauce or tamari and move the fuck on.

**** A 15-ounce can of chickpeas, drained and rinsed, is cool, too.

MAKES ½ CUP
(TRIPLE IT AND
KEEP THIS FUCKER
IN THE FRIDGE)

BASIC BALSAMIC AND WHITE WINE VINAIGRETTE

1 clove garlic, minced

1 teaspoon Dijon mustard

2 tablespoons balsamic vinegar

2 tablespoons white wine vinegar

¼ cup olive oil

Dress your Big-Ass Salad (page 91) with whatever the fuck you want, from our Low-Fat Farmhouse Dip (page 45), Italian Dressing (page 82), Creamy Avocado Lime Dressing (below), to this balsamic bastard.

Pour all this shit together in a jar and shake the fuck out of it. Taste and add more of whateverthefuck you think it needs. Refrigerate until go-time.

MAKES ABOUT
1 CUP

CREAMY AVOCADO LIME DRESSING

1 avocado

⅓ cup lime juice

¼ cup water

2 tablespoons rice vinegar

1 clove garlic, minced

¼ teaspoon ground cumin

Pinch of salt

2 tablespoons chopped cilantro (optional)

Make your friends see green when you whip out this clever-as-fuck dressing. And yeah, this is great on anything from a Big-Ass Salad (page 91) to leftover Breakfast Taco stuff (page 29) piled over some spinach.

Put all the ingredients in a blender or food processor and run it until everything looks all creamy, about 1 minute. If the dressing is too thick because you got an amazing avocado, add more water a tablespoon at a time until it's less like a dip and more like a goddamn dressing. Refrigerate until it is time to get dressed up.

BLENDER RED SAUCE

MAKES ABOUT
2½ CUPS

This simple son of a bitch makes a great pasta or dipping sauce with a little nooch and fresh basil, but it really fucking shines in the Italian Couscous Casserole (page 125). Whatever the hell you do with it, you won't be sorry.

2 red bell peppers, roasted (optional)*

1 can (15 ounces) no-salt-added tomato sauce

2 cloves garlic

Throw all that shit in a blender and run it until the sauce looks saucy. You know what the fuck that means. This will keep in the fridge for 2 weeks, no problem.

Optional, but way fucking worth it. Learn how to roast those fuckers up on page 217.

SRIRACHA AIOLI

MAKES ABOUT
2 CUPS

Sure this is tasty on a banh mi (page 164), but don't be afraid to slather the spicy son of bitch in your next taco, burrito, or burger. You'll never regret it.

12 ounces soft silken tofu*

¼ cup neutral oil, such as grapeseed

2 tablespoons Sriracha or similar style hot sauce

1 tablespoon lemon juice

1 teaspoon Dijon mustard

2 cloves garlic, minced

⅛ teaspoon salt

Throw everything together in a blender or food processor and run it until everything looks smooth and mixed up, about 1 minute. This flavorful motherfucker will keep in the fridge for about 2 weeks. If it starts to separate, just throw it back in the blender and emulsify its ass one more time.

Tofu got you all fucked up? See page 231.

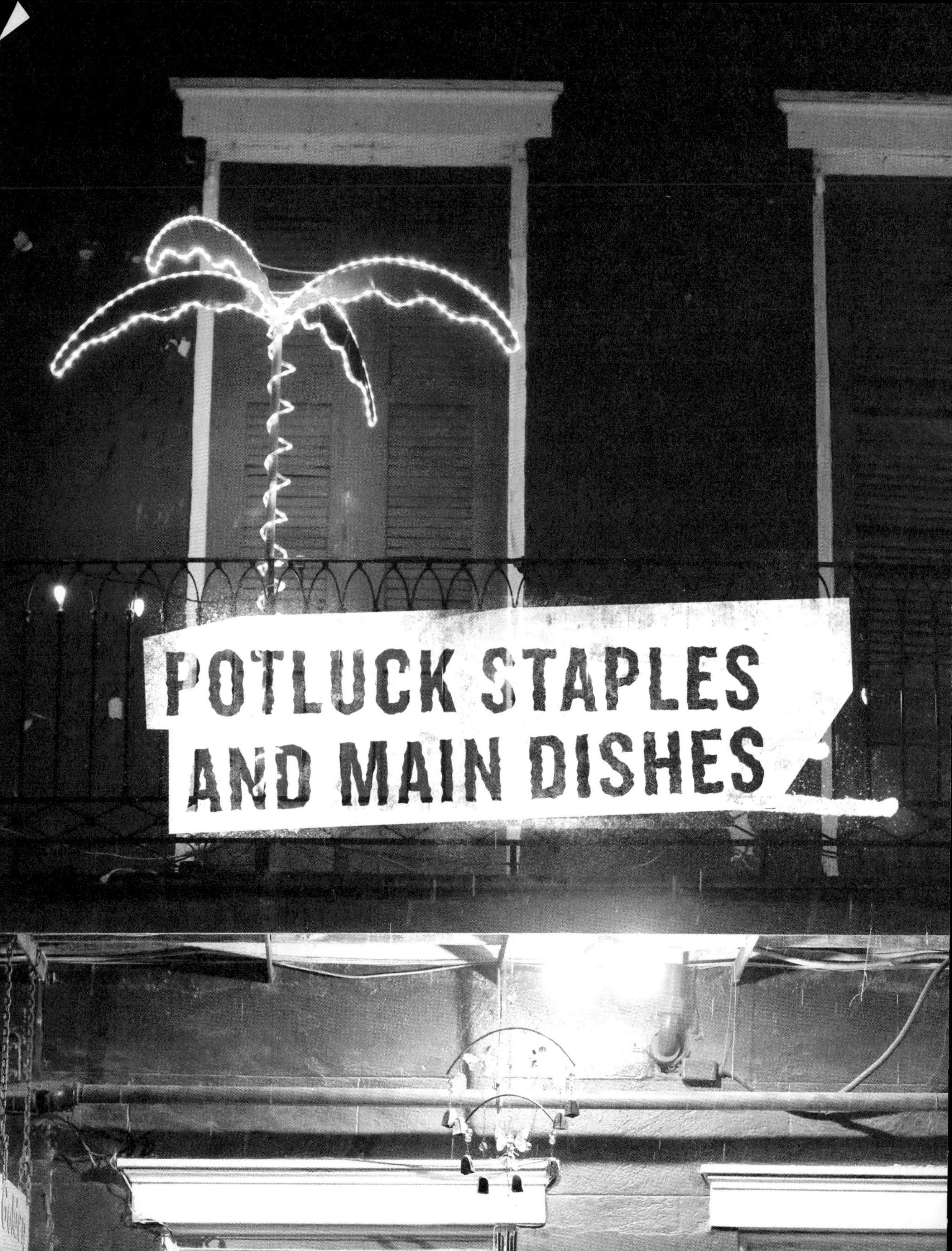

POTLUCK STAPLES AND MAIN DISHES

POTATO AND WHITE BEAN PIEROGIES
WITH CHEATER SAUERKRAUT

If you've never had a pierogi, then you have our condolences. These dumpling-ravioli hybrids have some delicious carb-on-carb action going on. These take a minute, but that shit is worth it. We came up with a quick sauerkraut-tasting dish to serve alongside, but if you have the real shit, use that. All those good probiotics in that fermented fucker can't be beat when it comes to what's good for your gut.

DOUGH

2½ cups all-purpose flour,* plus more for kneading

¼ teaspoon salt

¼ teaspoon garlic powder

1½ to 2 cups warm water

1 teaspoon olive oil

FILLING

1 pound red or yellow potatoes (about 4 fist-size potatoes)

2 teaspoons olive oil

½ large yellow onion, chopped

3 cups spinach, chopped

Salt

1½ cups cooked Great Northern or cannellini beans**

3 cloves garlic, minced

1 tablespoon lemon juice

2 teaspoons of your favorite vinegary hot sauce (like Tabasco)

2 tablespoons nooch***

Cheater Sauerkraut (page 115)

Nondairy sour cream

1 First, make the dough: In a large bowl, whisk together the flour, salt, and garlic powder. Stir in the warm water until a kinda sticky, shaggy ball of dough is formed. If there's still a bunch of dry flour in the bottom of the bowl or stuck all around the dough, add more water a tablespoon at a time and it will fix that shit. Throw some extra flour on your countertop so the dough won't stick, and dump that shit out on it. Knead for about 10 minutes until a nice smooth ball starts to form. Knead help kneading? (We're so sorry, it pained us to write it as much as it did for you to read it.) Check page 228 for the hot tips.

2 Put the kneaded ball of dough back in the bowl, coat it with the olive oil and stick that shit in a warm place, covered with a towel for 30 minutes, while you make the filling. It can wait up to 1½ hours, so it's fine if you cook a little slower.

(continued)

If you want to do a lot of the work ahead of time, make the dumplings all the way until the dough is still raw but the pierogies are all sealed. Spray them with some oil, cover them with plastic wrap, and fucking freeze them in a single layer on a baking sheet. This keeps those bastards from sticking together. When they're all frozen, dump them into a plastic bag or some Tupperware and store in the freezer for up to 3 months. BOOM. Tasty fucking food as an entrée or appetizer whenever the hell you want. When you're ready to get down, just boil them for an extra minute or two. Or if you're just spreading out the work, you could make the filling a day or two ahead of time. It keeps in the fridge for a couple days.

3 Make the filling: Chop the potatoes up into chunks no bigger than a poker chip. It's cool to leave the skin on if you're all about the fiber life. Place a steamer insert and a couple inches of water in a medium pot. Add the potatoes, cover, heat that shit over medium-low heat, and steam those tubers until you can stick a fork through with no fucking problem, 15 to 20 minutes.

4 While the potatoes are getting soft, grab a skillet and heat up the oil over medium heat. Add the onion and sauté that shit until it starts to brown, about 5 minutes. Add the spinach, a pinch of salt, and keep cooking until the spinach is all wilted down, about 2 minutes longer. Remove from the heat and leave that shit there.

5 Grab a large bowl and dump the beans in. Using a potato masher or a big-ass spoon, mash those motherfuckers up until a smoothish paste is formed. By now the potatoes should be down, so dump those spuds in and keep smashing until it kinda looks like mashed potatoes. Add the onion-spinach mixture, the garlic, lemon juice, hot sauce, and nooch and mix it up until it's all combined. Taste that starchy savior and add more garlic, lemon juice, hot sauce, or salt depending on whatthefuck you think is missing.

6 Fill a large pot with water and bring that shit to a boil over medium-high heat while you assemble the pierogies.

7 Flour the counter where you kneaded the dough again and grab half of the rested dough. Roll that shit out nice and thin, about the thickness of a tortilla. Grab a biscuit cutter or jar with a mouth at least 2½ inches wide and cut out some rounds for your pierogies. Ball up any scraps and reroll them. We usually get about 12 rounds for each half of dough. Grab the other half of the dough and repeat that shit.

8 To stuff the pierogies, grab a small glass of water and use your finger to wet the edges of each dough round. Add about 1 tablespoon of filling to each round and then fold that shit over. Seal the edges down with your finger and then crimp that shit with a fork so it looks kinda like a pie crust along the edges. Put them all on a floured baking sheet until you're all done and ready to boil them.

9 To cook, drop them down in the boiling water in batches no larger than 6 at a time so those fuckers don't all stick together. Boil them until they all start to float and the dough is cooked through, about 5 minutes. Fish them out with a slotted spoon, throw them on a plate, and keep boiling all the remaining pierogies.

10 Once the pierogies are all done, serve with a side of the sauerkraut and maybe some sour cream. Dig in and enjoy.

* You can try whole wheat pastry flour, but this is one of those times that all-purpose really just works best. It's the fucking truth.

** One 15-ounce can of beans, drained and rinsed, will do if you want to save yourself some extra work. You've earned that much, if you ask us.

*** WTF? See page 231.

CHEATER SAUERKRAUT

MAKES ABOUT 4 CUPS

1 Warm up a large skillet with a lid over medium heat. Add the cabbage and enough water for it to be about halfway submerged. Fold in the bay leaves, garlic, vinegar, sugar, and salt and bring that shit to a simmer.

2 Reduce the heat to medium-low, cover, and let that that fucker simmer until the cabbage gets kinda wilty, about 15 minutes. Uncover, increase the heat to medium, and simmer until the cabbage is all cooked through and most of the liquid is evaporated, about 15 minutes longer. If it's all cooked but there's still some water left, just drain that excess shit off, no stress.

3 Stir in the dill, discard the bay leaves, and stick the sauerkraut in the fridge until it cools down. Taste and add more garlic, dill, salt, or vinegar, whatever you think it needs to taste right. You can make this fiberful motherfucker a couple days in advice. Serve in a big-ass bowl alongside some pierogies and enjoy that shit.

6 cups shredded cabbage, red or green

4 bay leaves*

3 cloves garlic, minced

3 tablespoons apple cider vinegar

¼ teaspoon sugar

½ teaspoon salt

¼ cup chopped fresh dill (optional)**

* This shit is with the rest of the spices. Promise.

** Optional, but that is some deliciousness we wouldn't pass over. Also, dill can help soothe some of the cabbage's gassier tendencies. Just sayin'.

GET DOWN WITH THE
GOOD STUFF

WORTH-THE-MESS SLOPPY JOES

These saucy sons of bitches are so good that even the pickiest eaters will clean their plates. Just don't tell anyone there's veggies in there and you're good to go.

---

1 In a large skillet or wok, warm the oil over medium-high heat. Add the onion, bell pepper, and carrot and cook until they start to soften and the onion looks kinda translucent, about 4 minutes. Add the mushrooms and cook until the mushrooms start to soften up too, about 2 minutes longer.

2 Add the garlic, jalapeños, soy sauce or tamari, smoked paprika, cumin, and mustard powder and sauté until the mushrooms have released some of their liquid and everything is smelling fucking awesome, about 2 minutes.

3 Dump in the whole beans, lentils, tomato sauce, vinegar and bring that shit up to a simmer. Once everything is all warmed up, turn off the heat and taste that shit. Add more garlic, salt, spices— you know, flavor—if you think it needs a little extra something.

4 To serve, pile high on toasted burger buns with a side of celery seed slaw (from the BBQ Bean Sliders, page 127) or a Big-Ass Salad (page 91). End up with some leftovers? This also makes a thick but badass pasta sauce.

* You know what you can handle.

** Not like the mustard condiment, it's the kind you find on the spice aisle. No luck or don't want to spend the cash? Sub in 1 teaspoon of prepared yellow mustard if you must.

*** Or one 15-ounce can of beans, all rinsed and shit.

**** No fucking clue how to cook lentils? See Basic Pot of Beans, page 211.

***** One 15-ounce can of tomato sauce is cool here.

2 teaspoons olive oil

½ yellow onion, chopped (about 1 cup)

1 red or green bell pepper, chopped (about 1 cup)

1 carrot, chopped (about ½ cup)

1 cup finely chopped button or cremini mushrooms

2 cloves garlic, minced

1 to 2 jalapeños,* seeded and minced

2 teaspoons soy sauce or tamari

2 teaspoons smoked paprika

1 teaspoon ground cumin

1 teaspoon mustard powder**

1½ cups cooked kidney beans***

1½ cups cooked lentils (about ¾ cup dried)****

1½ cups tomato sauce*****

1 tablespoon apple cider vinegar or lemon juice

4 or 6 whole wheat hamburger buns, split and toasted

SHAVED ASPARAGUS PIZZA

½ batch Everyday Pizza
Dough (page 226)

Roasted Garlic White
Sauce (opposite)

1 pound asparagus

1 tablespoon lemon juice

1 teaspoon olive oil

Pinch of salt

Olive oil, for brushing
the crust

Toppings: arugula,
chopped chives or green
onions, lemon juice

Hot sauce, for serving

There are a shitload of pizza options out
there but if you've never tried asparagus,
you're seriously missing out. Once the raw
asparagus gets roasted up with the dough
some real magical shit happens, with
delicious results.

1 Make the pizza dough through step 4. While that yeasty beast
is rising, make the garlic sauce and start the oven cranking to
475°F. Cook this on a chilly day and give your heater a fucking
break.

2 Grab your asparagus and chop the bottom inch off all the
spears. That shit is just too tough and you look like a fucking
rabbit trying to chew a veggie for that long. Grab a single spear,
hold it down on a cutting board, and use your vegetable peeler to
peel off a long strip, like you are peeling a carrot. Do each side a
couple of times until you are left with a kinda thin strip. Do this
with all the spears. You don't need to be perfect—you just are
looking for mostly thin strips. Throw the shaved asparagus in a
medium bowl and mix it up with the lemon juice, oil, and salt. It
might look like way too much shit for 2 pizzas, but these fibrous
bastards will shrink down once they hit the oven. Trust.

3 Roll out one ball of the dough using the deets on page 227.
Spread a bunch of the roasted garlic sauce down over your pizza-
shaped dough, and pile on about half the asparagus, leaving
1 inch around the edges as the crust. (Did you really need a
reminder to leave space for crust on a pizza? We fucking hope
not.) Repeat with the second ball of dough.

4 Brush those crusts with olive oil, put on a baking sheet, and bake until the crusts look golden, 10 to 12 minutes. Pile on some arugula, some chives, and a little more lemon juice and serve that shit up hot with some hot sauce on the side.

ROASTED GARLIC WHITE SAUCE

Throw the flour, oil, milk, roasted garlic, and nooch into a blender and run that fucker until the roasted garlic is all chopped up and the sauce looks mostly smooth. Pour all that in a small saucepan and warm it up over medium heat, whisking it every few minutes until that shit starts to thicken up, about 5 minutes. Whisk in the lemon juice and salt, then turn the heat off.

* No fucking clue how to roast garlic? See page 217.

** WTF? See page 231.

MAKES ABOUT 1¼ CUPS

3 tablespoons whole wheat pastry or all-purpose flour

1 tablespoon olive oil

1½ cups unsweetened nondairy milk

2 bulbs garlic, roasted*

2 tablespoons nooch**

2 teaspoons lemon juice

¼ teaspoon salt

THANK YOU FOR YOUR BUSINESS

MADE JUST FOR YO

1 **Buffalo Pizza**
(page 122)

2 **Shaved Asparagus Pizza** (page 118)

3 **A Goddamn Mess**

½ batch Everyday Pizza
Dough (page 226)

BUFFALO TEMPEH
1 tablespoon all-purpose
or whole wheat pastry
flour

1 tablespoon apple
cider vinegar

¾ cup hot sauce*

2 teaspoons olive oil

8 ounces tempeh,
crumbled**

¼ cup chopped yellow
onion

1 clove garlic, minced

WHITE SAUCE
3 tablespoons all-
purpose flour

2 tablespoons olive oil

1½ cups unsweetened
nondairy milk

1 clove garlic, chopped

¼ teaspoon salt

2 tablespoons nooch***

¼ teaspoon dried basil

¼ teaspoon dried dill

¼ teaspoon celery
seed****

1 tablespoon lemon juice

Olive oil, for brushing
the crust

TOPPINGS
1 cup finely chopped
celery

½ avocado, chopped

1 tablespoon lemon juice

Pinch of salt

Chopped chives
(optional)

Hot sauce, for serving

BUFFALO PIZZA

Sure, it looks like a lot of fucking steps to make a pizza, but it's totally worth it. Plus, this is easy shit and most of it can be done ahead of time if you like to plan out your pizza parties like a fucking champ.

———————————————————

1 Make the pizza dough on page 226 through step 3. While that yeasty beast is rising, make all your toppings and crank up the oven to 475°F. Yeah, your kitchen is going to be hot as fuck, but you're getting pizza out of it. Fair trade.

2 Now get that buffalo tempeh going: In a small glass, mix together the flour and vinegar until you get a paste. Slowly whisk in that hot sauce and try to minimize the chunks. Set that spicy son of a bitch aside.

3 Warm up the oil in a large skillet or wok over medium heat. Add the crumbled tempeh and onion and sauté that shit around until they both look a little golden in some spots, 5 to 7 minutes. Add the garlic and then pour over the hot sauce mixture. Stir this all around and let it cook for about 1 minute so that the tempeh absorbs a little bit of the sauce, then turn that heat right off. Yeah, your whole place smells like hot sauce now. YOU'RE FUCKING WELCOME.

4 To make the white sauce: Throw the flour, oil, milk, garlic, salt, and nooch in a blender and run that fucker until the garlic is all chopped up and the sauce looks mostly smooth. Pour all of that into a small saucepan and add the dried herbs. Warm it all up over medium heat, whisking it every few minutes until that shit starts to thicken up, about 5 minutes. Whisk in the lemon juice and remove from the heat.

5 Roll out one ball of dough using the instructions back on page 227. Spread a bunch of the white sauce down over your pizza-shaped dough, and pile on about half the buffaloed tempeh, leaving about 1 inch around the edges as the crust. Do the same shit with the rest of the dough, white sauce, and tempeh.

6 Brush those crusts with olive oil, put those pies on a baking sheet, and bake until the crusts look golden, 10 to 12 minutes.

7 While the pizzas are baking, set up the toppings: Mix up the celery and avocado in a small bowl with the lemon juice and salt.

8 When the pizzas are done, sprinkle the celery-avocado mixture all over the pies and drizzle on some more of the white sauce if you have some left. You can toss on some chopped chives if you're feeling fancy but that shit isn't necessary. Serve right away with some extra hot sauce on the side.

* Frank's RedHot is traditional, but do whatever basic vinegar red hot sauce you can find at the store.

** Just crumble this fermented fucker right into the pan into pieces no bigger than a dime. Not sure what tempeh is? See page 231.

*** WTF? See page 231.

**** Celery seed is in the spice aisle with the other spices. We fucking promise. It's been there forever. Not some new, weird trendy shit you have to hunt down. It's old school.

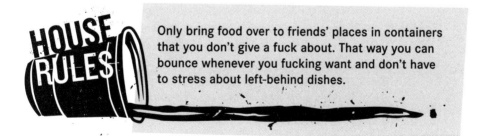

HOUSE RULES

Only bring food over to friends' places in containers that you don't give a fuck about. That way you can bounce whenever you fucking want and don't have to stress about left-behind dishes.

FRESH TOMATO AND PESTO PIZZA

This pizza is just fancy enough to impress a crowd but familiar enough to not scare off any culinary cowards.

½ batch Everyday Pizza Dough (page 226)

PESTO

2½ cups packed torn basil leaves

⅔ cup slivered or sliced almonds

¼ cup olive oil

¼ cup water

¾ teaspoon grated lemon zest*

2 tablespoons lemon juice

½ teaspoon salt

2 to 3 cloves garlic, chopped, depending on your love of garlic

TOPPINGS

Roasted Garlic White Sauce (page 119)

2 large tomatoes, sliced into thin half-moons

Olive oil, for brushing the crust

Hot sauce, for serving

Need help zesting? See page 218.

1 Make the pizza dough on page 226 through step 4. Start cranking up the oven to 475°F. Yeah, you're using that hot hot heat.

2 While that yeasty beast is rising, make the pesto: Put all the ingredients in a food processor or blender and blend until smooth-ish. Scrape the pesto out of the processor. (No food processor? Don't give up, adapt and improvise, motherfucker. Just put the almonds in a plastic bag and smash them until they're tiny and chop the rest of that shit up supersmall too. Mix all of it together with a fork until it looks like a paste.) Set the pesto aside.

3 After you make the pesto, rinse the processor or blender out and use it to make the roasted garlic sauce. Easy shit.

4 Roll out one ball of the dough using the instructions on page 227. Spread about ¼ cup of the roasted garlic sauce down over your dough, and then smear a good amount of pesto over that shit, leaving about 1 inch around the edges as the crust. Lay down the tomato slices all over that and drizzle some roasted garlic sauce over the top. Repeat that shit with the second ball of dough.

5 Brush the crusts with olive oil, put that shit on a baking sheet, and bake until the crusts look golden, 10 to 12 minutes. If you have extra pesto, dollop some of that shit on top before serving.

6 Serve hot, with some hot sauce on the side if you like a little fire on your 'za.

ITALIAN COUSCOUS CASSEROLE

This isn't the prettiest dish in the book but what it lacks in looks, it more than makes up in flavor. Not only that but it's easy as hell to throw together and will keep in the fridge no problem, so you can get down on this motherfucker all week if you're riding solo.

1 Crank up the oven to 375°F. Grease a 9 x 9 x 3-inch baking dish (or smaller as long as it is at least 3 inches deep).

2 In a large wok or skillet, warm up the olive oil over medium-high heat. Throw the eggplant and onion into the pan and sauté until the onion starts looking a little translucent, 3 to 4 minutes. Add the squash, garlic, thyme, basil, and red pepper flakes (if using) and sauté for 2 more minutes. Fold in the spinach, salt, couscous, red sauce, vinegar, and lemon juice. Sauté for another minute or two to wilt the spinach. Remove from the heat and stir in the nooch. Taste and add more garlic or whatever the fuck you think it needs.

3 Scrape the mixture into the baking dish. Cover it with foil and bake for 20 minutes. Uncover and bake until the edges look golden and tasty as hell, about 15 minutes longer. Serve right away with some fresh basil or parsley on top so it looks pro.

* Optional, but fucking awesome.

** Learn how to cook that couscous shit on page 213.

*** WTF? See page 231.

2 teaspoons olive oil

1 medium eggplant, unpeeled, cut into chunks (about 3 cups)

1 medium yellow onion, chopped

1 medium yellow squash or zucchini, shredded (about 1½ cups)

2 cloves garlic, minced

2 teaspoons dried thyme

2 teaspoons dried basil

¼ teapsoon red pepper flakes (optional)*

2 cups chopped spinach

½ teaspoon salt

3 cups cooked couscous (1¼ cups uncooked)**

Blender Red Sauce (page 107)

2 tablespoons red wine vinegar

2 tablespoons lemon juice

½ cup nooch***

Chopped fresh basil or parsley for garnish (optional)

BRO-DOWN
THROW DOWN

Throw on your favorite sleeveless shirt and crack open some cold ones because these dishes got your back, bro (or part-time bro). Whether you're gathering for the game or settling scores in beer pong, these recipes are a satisfying ensemble to your brocial club gathering.

BBQ BEAN SLIDERS WITH CELERY SEED SLAW

It's not like BBQ sliders need help selling themselves, but this slaw takes these bite-size bastards to another level. Just make copies of this page now because people are going to be asking you for the recipe all damn day. Or tell them to buy their own fucking book.

---

1 Warm the oven to 425°F. Lightly grease a large baking sheet.

2 Make the burgers: Add the beans to a large bowl and mash those fuckers up with a potato masher or large spoon until a sorta paste forms. A couple of larger bean chunks are cool. Add the zucchini, onion, garlic, oil, soy sauce or tamari, liquid smoke, and seasoning blend and mix until it's all distributed. Fold in the bread crumbs and stir that shit around until there are no dry patches and everything is uniform. This should feel slightly sticky and hold nicely when you form it into a ball. If it is too wet, add more bread crumbs. Too dry? Add some fucking oil. Stop looking for excuses why you're a bad cook. Taste and add more spices and whatever until it tastes good enough to you. Can't do that shit with ground beef.

3 Form the mixture into 12 patties if you are making sliders or 6 patties if you are making regular burgers. Whateverthefuck you wanna do. Place them on the baking sheet, spray them lightly with oil, and bake, flipping halfway, until they look a little golden brown, 35 to 40 minutes. If you're doing full-size burgers you might need to let them go 10 extra minutes.

(continued)

BURGERS
3 cups cooked kidney beans*

1½ cups grated zucchini (about 2 medium)

½ medium onion, chopped (about ½ cup)

2 cloves garlic, minced

1 tablespoon olive oil

2 teaspoons soy sauce or tamari

2 teaspoons liquid smoke**

1 teaspoon of your favorite no-salt, all-purpose seasoning blend

½ cup bread crumbs***

Spray oil

CELERY SEED SLAW
½ pound cabbage, sliced into thin strips (about 4 cups)

1 carrot, shredded (about ¼ cup)

¼ cup finely chopped green onions

¼ teaspoon salt

3 tablespoons rice vinegar

1 tablespoon olive or grapeseed oil

¼ teaspoon celery seed****

Quick Homemade BBQ Sauce (page 93) or your favorite shit from the store

12 slider buns or 6 regular buns

4 While the burgers are baking, make the slaw: In a medium bowl, combine the cabbage, carrot, green onions, and salt. Get your hands in there and kinda massage the salt into the cabbage. This will help your slaw soften up faster so that your whole burger is on point. Add the vinegar, oil, and celery seed and stir that shit up so everything is coated. Stick that shit in the fridge to chill until go-time.

5 To assemble the burgers, coat the patties with BBQ sauce and smear a good amount on both sides of the buns. There's no such thing as too much BBQ sauce. Pile a good amount of slaw right on top of that saucyass patty and you're ready to get down. Serve within an hour of assembling so that your bun isn't a sad soggy pile of mush.

* Two 15-ounce cans, drained and rinsed, are totally fine. Black beans would be a good sub too.

** Calm the fuck down, we explain that shit on page 231.

*** Any kind of regular bread crumbs you have are fine. Got nothing? Just toast up some bread until it is almost burnt looking and real dry, then grate it or put it in a food processor to get some tiny fucking crumbs. They help soak up all the liquid, so DO NOT leave this shit out.

**** Clueless? See page 123.

WHEN YOU WANT MULTIPLE BURGERS WITHOUT THE SHAME OF KEEPING COUNT

YIPPEE PAELLA MOTHERFUCKER

SUMMER NIGHT PAELLA

This fancy motherfucker is the dish to make if you've got something to prove. Make sure you get everything ready before you start cooking and you'll have this shit done, no problem. At the end of the day you're just cooking some rice, so don't let that shake you.

---

1 In a medium pot, combine the broth and wine and warm up to a gentle simmer over medium-low heat. Add the saffron, cover, and turn off the heat. Let the saffron steep while you get the rest of your shit together.

2 In a 14- to 18-inch skillet or paella pan, warm up the olive oil over medium heat. Add the onion and sauté until the onion gets kinda translucent and sweaty, about 3 minutes. Add the mushrooms, tomatoes, and salt and sauté until most of the liquid has evaporated from the pan, like another 4 to 5 minutes. Add the lima beans, garlic, and smoked paprika and sauté for 30 seconds, just so that everything gets mixed up. Add the rice and cook it just long enough to make sure it gets mixed with all the veggies.

3 Quickly fish out the saffron threads from the broth and toss them. RIP you overpriced bastards. Pour the warm broth over the rice mixture, stir it once to make sure everything is all evenly distributed, and scrape down the sides to get all the stragglers. Bring the pan to a strong simmer, cover, and reduce the heat to medium-low. (No lid for your pot? Use some foil or a nonwarped cookie sheet to cover that shit like we do.) Let that softly simmer for about 25 minutes.

(continued)

2½ cups vegetable broth

¾ cup dry white wine*

Pinch of saffron threads**

1 tablespoon olive oil

½ medium yellow onion, chopped (about 1 cup)

¾ cup chopped button or cremini mushrooms

2 large tomatoes, chopped

¼ teaspoon salt

1 cup frozen lima beans***

3 cloves garlic, minced

1½ teaspoons smoked paprika

1½ cups short- or medium-grain white rice****

4 spears asparagus, halved lengthwise

1 red bell pepper, roasted (see page 217), cut into strips

1 can (14 ounces) water-packed artichoke hearts, drained, rinsed, and quartered

2 tablespoons lemon juice

Paprika, for garnish

4 After 25 minutes, uncover the paella and arrange the asparagus, bell pepper, and artichoke hearts on top in whatever badass pattern of your choosing. Express yourself goddammit. Press them gently into the rice just a little bit and keep that shit cooking until all the water is absorbed in the pan and it starts to smell kinda toasty, about 10 minutes longer.

5 Drizzle with the lemon juice and shake a little paprika over the top for looks and let that gorgeous carb queen cool for about 10 minutes before serving.

* Whatever the fuck you plan to drink later will work here. Don't do wine? Just add the same amount of broth.

** Saffron is expensive as all hell. We kept it in the recipe because of tradition, but don't let that shit stop you. If you can't find it/don't want to spend a fuck-ton of cash on it, just leave the saffron out. Your rice won't be as golden as the picture, but it will still be goddamn delicious.

*** Lima beans get a bad rap. Grab these tasty fuckers from the freezer section and diversify your bean game. Can't find them? Edamame or even green peas will do as a stand-in.

**** Bomba rice is traditional in paella but good luck finding that shit. Arborio will do just fine.

GRILLED PINEAPPLE AND SWEET-AND-SOUR TEMPEH KEBABS

So the process here is really similar to the other kebabs on page 136, but with, you know, completely different fucking flavors. These are great with the Pad Thai Rolls (page 40), Cold Noodle and Herb Salad (page 80), and a side of brown rice (see page 212). Or you could just eat them alone. In the dark. In front of your computer. Reading your own blog.

---

1 First, make the sweet-and-sour sauce: Mix the water and cornstarch together in a small bowl and set that shit aside. We are going to use the cornstarch later to make the sauce all thick and glossy and if you just add that fucker straight in without mixing it up in some liquid you just get a chunky disaster. Like shoes in the '90s.

2 In a medium saucepot, combine the pineapple juice, vinegar, lime juice, brown sugar, tomato paste, soy sauce or tamari, Sriracha, and garlic. Bring it to a simmer and cook for about 3 minutes, then whisk in the cornstarch mixture and simmer for another minute or two until it thickens up, then turn off the heat. You'll be amazed by how fucking easy it is and feel real dumb for ever buying a jar of sweet-and-sour. Real fucking dumb. Let this sit covered on the stovetop while you get everything else ready.

(continued)

SWEET-AND-SOUR SAUCE
2 tablespoons water

2 tablespoons cornstarch

1 cup pineapple juice

¼ cup rice vinegar

1 tablespoon lime juice

1 tablespoon brown sugar

2 teaspoons tomato paste

2 teaspoons soy sauce or tamari

2 teaspoons Sriracha or similar-style hot sauce

2 cloves garlic, sliced

KEBABS
8 ounces tempeh,* cut into large cubes

½ cup vegetable broth

2 tablespoons rice vinegar

1 tablespoon soy sauce or tamari

1 tablespoon olive or grapeseed oil

½ red or white onion

1 bell pepper, any color

2 cups fresh or canned pineapple chunks

10 bamboo or wooden skewers

Spray oil

1 Grilled Pineapple
and Sweet-and-Sour
Tempeh Kebabs
(page 133)

2 Grilled Veggie and
Tempeh Kebabs with
Chimichurri Sauce
(page 136)

3 Some Dangerous Shit
You Should Never Do

3 For the kebabs: Place a steamer insert and a couple inches of water in a small pot. Bring to a boil over medium heat. Add the tempeh, cover, and steam until it starts to smell kinda nutty, about 10 minutes.

4 While the tempeh is steaming, mix the broth, vinegar, soy sauce or tamari, and oil together in a medium bowl.

5 When the tempeh is done, dump it into the bowl with the broth mixture and mix it together so every piece gets some of that flavor on it. Let it sit, stirring occasionally, while you chop the veggies.

6 Cut the onion and bell pepper into large chunks about the size of the tempeh cubes. Stick them, the pineapple, and the tempeh on the skewers alternating ingredients until you fill them all up. Like you are making a kebab, since that's what you are fucking doing.

7 Bring your grill to a medium-high heat.

8 Using a pastry brush or spoon, spread a little bit of the sweet-and-sour sauce over the kebabs. Yeah, it's gonna be a little messy, but fucking get over it. Spray them lightly with a little oil and head out to the grill. Place the kebabs on the grill and cook for 7 to 9 minutes, turning every couple minutes. You are looking for those bomb-ass grill marks and for the veggies to get golden brown around the edges. If they start looking a little dry before they are done, brush them with a little bit of sweet-and-sour sauce. Take them off the grill, brush with a little more sauce, and let them cool for a bit.

9 Serve warm and watch everyone start asking when the fuck you ran out for takeout. Accept tips.

* WTF? See page 231.

GRILLED VEGGIE AND TEMPEH KEBABS WITH CHIMICHURRI SAUCE

These smoky sons of bitches are filled with marinated tempeh and served up with a green sauce that packs enough flavor to make your fucking head explode. Literally. Just dead. Anyways, chimichurri sauce is crazy popular in Argentina and once you whip it up you'll understand why. You can even forget the kebabs and just pour some sauce on everything. Brush your fucking teeth with it. Who cares. Life is meaningless. None of this matters.

CHIMICHURRI SAUCE
1 cup chopped fresh flat-leaf parsley
¼ cup chopped shallot or white onion
¼ cup olive oil
3 tablespoons red wine vinegar
2 tablespoons water
1 tablespoon lemon juice
1 tablespoon chopped fresh oregano
3 cloves garlic, chopped
1 serrano pepper, seeded and chopped
¼ teaspoon salt

KEBABS
8 ounces tempeh,* cut into large cubes
½ cup vegetable broth
1 tablespoon soy sauce or tamari
1 tablespoon liquid smoke*
1 tablespoon olive or grapeseed oil
2 small zucchini or yellow squash
½ red or white onion
1 red bell pepper
10 bamboo or wooden skewers
2 teaspoons of your favorite no-salt, all-purpose seasoning
¼ teaspoon paprika**

1 Make the chimichurri sauce: Throw all the sauce ingredients together in a food processor or blender and let that fucker run until it looks kinda like a chunky pesto. If it's getting a little stuck, add a tablespoon of water to get that shit going again.

2 For the kebabs: Place a steamer insert and a couple inches of water in a small pot. Bring to a boil over medium heat. Add the tempeh, cover, and steam until it starts to smell kinda nutty, about 10 minutes.

3 While the tempeh is steaming, mix the broth, soy sauce or tamari, liquid smoke, and oil together is a medium bowl.

4 When the tempeh is done, dump it in the bowl with the marinade and mix it together so every piece gets some of that flavor on it. Let it sit, stirring occasionally, while you chop the veggies.

5 Cut the zucchini, onion, and bell pepper into large chunks about the size of the tempeh cubes. Stick them and the tempeh on the skewers alternating ingredients until you fill them all up. You know what the fuck to do; you've seen a fucking kebab before. (Don't throw the tempeh marinade out.)

6 Bring your grill to a medium-high heat.

7 In a small bowl, mix together 2 tablespoons of that tempeh marinade, the no-salt seasoning, and the paprika. Using a pastry brush or spoon, spread that shit all over the kebabs. That's right, we're layering the flavors, bitches. Place the kebabs on the grill and cook for 7 to 9 minutes, turning every couple minutes. You are looking for those bomb-ass grill marks and for the veggies to get golden brown around the edges. If they start looking a little dry before they are done, brush them with a little bit of olive oil or some of the remaining marinade. Take them off the grill and let them cool for a hot minute.

8 To serve you can either pour the chimichurri sauce over the kebabs or serve it on the side so people can dip how they want. Up to you. Or forget other people and just make these for yourself. B.Y.O.K.

* WTF? See page 231.

** Paprika is just so it looks extra sexy. Leave it out if you don't already have that shit in your pantry.

HOUSE RULES

If you're using bamboo or wooden skewers, soak those motherfuckers in some water for at least 10 minutes before you start grilling. This will keep the ends from burning up as soon as you set them on the grill. That shit is amateur.

8 ounces tempeh*

BACON-ISH MARINADE
1½ cups vegetable broth

¼ cup soy sauce or
tamari**

2 tablespoons apple
cider vinegar

2 tablespoons liquid
smoke***

1 tablespoon blackstrap
molasses****

1 teaspoon smoked
paprika

1 teaspoon onion powder

3 cloves garlic, sliced

1 tablespoon olive oil

Lettuce

Sliced tomatoes,
avocado, and red onion

8 slices bread, like
sourdough, toasted*****

Dijon mustard

* WTF? See page 231.

** Calm the fuck down. It's a
marinade, not a fucking drink.
You won't be consuming that
much sodium, we swear.

*** WTF? See page 231.

**** Confused? See the
House Rule on page 93.

***** We're not gonna
fucking tell you how to make
toast. Forget it.

TLTA SAMMIES

These sammies are equal part smoky
deliciousness and crunchy veggie goodness.
Just go ahead and double the recipe for the
tempeh now because we know goddamn well
you're gonna want leftovers.

1 Slice the tempeh into planks about ¼ inch thick and 2 inches
long. No need to fucking measure it out, just trust your 3rd grade
teacher did an okay job with you and fucking eyeball it.

2 Next, make the bacon-ish marinade: Stir the broth, soy sauce
or tamari, vinegar, liquid smoke, molasses, paprika, onion powder,
and garlic together in a shallow dish, like a pie pan or some shit.
Add the tempeh planks gently to the dish so you don't splash
everywhere and then just give up. The tempeh won't all be
covered, but just fucking make it work the best you can. Cover
that up and stick it in the fridge to marinate for at least 2 hours
and up to 8. Yeah, you'd better have read this shit all the way
through before you started cooking hungry.

3 When the tempeh is ready, in a large skillet or wok, heat up the
oil over medium heat. Lay the tempeh planks down in a single
layer and cook them until they start to brown, 2 to 3 minutes on
each side. When it starts to look a little dry in there, or if the
tempeh feels like it might be sticking, just add a couple spoonfuls
of the marinade to keep it all movin'.

4 Once the tempeh is browned on both sides, you are ready to
make a badass sandwich. Pile lettuce, tomato, avocado, and red
onions onto your favorite toasted bread with a little mustard. It's
a fucking sandwich. If you get this far in the recipe but fail at the
assembling-a-sandwich part, then we honestly don't know what
the fuck to say to you.

DON'T OUTSOURCE
YOUR PARTY SAMMIES
TO SOME SUBWAY SWINDLER

TEX-MEX ENCHILADAS

Pinto beans, corn, and avocados are the building blocks of any Southwestern dish. But in this crowd-pleaser, it's more of a ménage à trois. Enchiladas have never been so Texy.

RANCHERO SAUCE
2 teaspoons olive oil

1 yellow onion, finely chopped

1 small green bell pepper, finely chopped

2 jalapeños, seeded and finely chopped*

1 clove garlic, minced

2 teaspoons ground cumin

¼ teaspoon salt

1½ cups vegetable broth

1 can (15 ounces) tomato sauce**

¼ cup chopped cilantro

1 tablespoon lime juice

FILLING
½ yellow onion

2 cloves garlic

3 cups cooked pinto beans***

¼ teaspoon ground cumin

¼ teaspoon salt

2 cups fresh or frozen corn kernels

2 avocados

2 teaspoons lime juice

8 flour or corn tortillas

1 Make the ranchero sauce: In a medium saucepan, warm up the oil over medium heat. Add the onion and bell pepper and cook them all up until the onion starts to look a little brown, 5 to 7 minutes. Add the jalapeños, garlic, cumin, and salt and sauté all that delicious shit around for another minute. Add the broth and tomato sauce and let that all simmer together until it starts to thicken up a little bit, 20 to 30 minutes. Like it will look more like a sauce and less like a bunch of fucking water, you know? Add the cilantro and lime juice and turn off the heat. Taste and add more garlic, cumin, lime juice, salt, whatever you think it's missing. Leave this motherfucker covered on the stovetop while you're making the rest of the enchiladas, or stick it in the fridge and use it up sometime that week. This should make about 3 cups.

2 To make the filling: Throw ½ cup of the ranchero sauce you just made into a blender or food processor. Add the onion, garlic, beans, cumin, and salt and run that shit until it all looks kinda smooth like bean dip. Pour that into a bowl and stir in the corn. Yeah, it looks all kinds of gross, but fucking move past it because it's going in enchiladas so you won't fucking see it. In a separate bowl, mash together the avocado and lime juice until you get it kinda smooth too. Done.

3 Now you're finally going to make the fucking enchiladas. Crank your oven up to 375°F. Grab a 9 x 13-inch baking dish.

4 Cover the bottom of the dish with about 1½ cups of ranchero sauce. Using a griddle, your oven, or the microwave, warm up the tortillas. Kinda dip the tortilla around in a little of the sauce in the dish so that the bottom side is all coated. Add a couple of spoonfuls of the bean corn filling in a line in the middle of the tortilla, throw some of the mashed avocado over the top, roll it up, and set it seam side down in the baking dish. You fucking know how enchiladas are supposed to look, so just do that shit. Keep going until you run out of space or out of filling.

5 Cover the enchiladas with the remaining ranchero sauce, cover the dish tightly with foil, and throw it in the oven for 20 minutes. Take off the foil and cook it for 5 more. Let it cool for a minute or two before serving.

* If you know your mouth is weak as shit, leave the jalapeños out or just use one.

** Not jarred pasta sauce . . . canned unseasoned tomato sauce. Try to get one low in sodium if you can. (Unintended can joke. Just chuckle softly to yourself and get back to cooking, goddammit.)

*** Yeah, just grab two 15-ounce cans of beans. We know what you're about. Just drain and rinse them.

HOUSE RULES

Put some random shit in your medicine cabinet to make nosy motherfuckers wonder what kind of lifestyle you're into. Ideas include: soy sauce packets, a melon baller, some old-timey photos of strangers (check your local flea market), and literally any office supplies. The rumors will start themselves!

1 cup vegetable broth

¼ cup apple cider vinegar

2 tablespoons rice vinegar

2 tablespoons soy sauce, tamari, or Bragg's*

½ teaspoon liquid smoke*

1 tablespoon paprika

2 teaspoons mustard powder or ground mustard seed

½ teaspoon garlic powder

½ teaspoon ground coriander**

¼ teaspoon finely ground black pepper

2 tablespoons olive oil

8 medium carrots, peeled, skinny end trimmed off, and cut the length of the buns

8 hotdog buns, whatever kind of shit you like

Topping ideas: smoky onions (from Cobb Salad, page 104), your favorite chili, dill relish, mustard, ketchup

CARROT DOGS

We heard there was a place called Fritzi Dog here in LA that served carrot hot dogs. We were ready to fucking mock that nonsense until we tried them and ended up ordering two more. So this is our simpler, homemade version for when the craving hits but we aren't willing to fight traffic. Don't be so quick to count out a carrot.

1 In a medium saucepan, mix together the broth, vinegars, soy sauce, liquid smoke, and spices. Bring that shit to a simmer while you throw the oil and the carrots together in a 9 x 13-inch baking dish. Let the marinade simmer for 5 minutes, then pour it over the carrots. Cover that shit with foil and let it sit for at least 30 minutes but up to 1½ hours.

2 When you are about ready to get these fuckers cooking, heat up your oven to 425°F.

3 Stick the carrots in the oven, still covered in foil, and cook them for 20 minutes. Then take off the foil, kinda stir them around/flip them over, and roast them for another 20 to 25 minutes. You want them to be tender on the outside with a little bit of resistance in the center when you stab one with a fork.

4 Add your choice of toppings and serve right away. Or stash them away and heat them back up on a well-oiled grill.

WTF? See page 231.

**Can't find that shit in the store/don't want to look? Leave it out.*

Socal Gourmet
Carrot Dogs

SOCAL GOURMET CARROT DOGS

Carrot Dogs (page 142)

Cilantro Pesto (below)

8 hotdog buns, whatever you like

2 avocados, sliced

3 jalapeños, sliced into thin rounds

Your favorite pico de gallo–style salsa*

If you really want to dress these beta-carotene bitches up something special here is our absolute favorite way to eat them. Sure, it's more work than just squirting ketchup all over them, but hot damn it's worth it.

_____

1 Make the carrot dogs and pesto.

2 To assemble a dog, smear some pesto on the inside of a bun, lay down a couple slices of avocado and jalapeño, and top the damn thing off with some salsa. Add more pesto if you are feeling extra fancy. Yeah we know this sounds fucked up, but you'll love this shit. We swear.

The salsa in our first book is the shit, just sayin'.

CILANTRO PESTO

2 cups chopped cilantro (about 1 big bunch)

½ cup slivered or sliced almonds

2 to 3 cloves garlic, chopped

½ teaspoon grated lemon zest*

1 tablespoon lemon juice

¼ teaspoon salt

¼ cup olive oil

¼ cup vegetable broth or water

Throw the cilantro, almonds, garlic, lemon zest, lemon juice, salt, oil, and broth in a food processor and blend until sorta smooth and, you know, pesto looking. No food processor? Just put the almonds in a bag and smash them until they are tiny and chop the rest of that shit up supersmall too. Mix all of it together with a fork until it looks like a paste.

WTF? See page 218.

VEGETABLE POT PIES

MAKES 4 INDIVIDUAL
POT PIES OR ONE
9-INCH PIE

Pot pies get treated like you're settling for something instead of the rock stars that they are. Forget those frozen store-bought pies of cardboard, because nothing comes even remotely close to a homemade pot pie. This comfort-food classic is perfect for a dinner party or even as an entrée on Thanksgiving.

½ batch Olive Oil Crust (page 225)

FILLING
2 teaspoons olive oil
½ yellow onion, chopped
1 carrot, chopped
1 cup frozen peas
¼ teaspoon salt
¼ teaspoon dried oregano
¼ teaspoon dried thyme
¼ teaspoon black pepper
2 cloves garlic, minced
¼ cup all-purpose flour
½ cup white wine*
2 cups vegetable broth
1½ cups cooked navy or white beans**
1 teaspoon lemon juice
1 tablespoon chopped fresh chives***
1 tablespoon chopped fresh parsley***

Olive oil, for brushing the crust

1 Make the pie crust on page 225 through step 2. Let it chill out in the fridge while you make the filling. Also, start cranking your oven to 425°F while you are at it. Decide if you're using a 9-inch pie pan or individual ramekins that hold about 2 cups to bake this shit. Get whatever you are going to use out and set it to the side.

2 To make the filling: In a medium saucepan, heat up the olive oil over medium heat. Add the onion and sauté until it starts looking golden and delicious, 5 to 7 minutes. Add the carrot and peas and keep cooking that shit for 2 more minutes so everything starts warming up. Add the salt, oregano, thyme, pepper, and garlic and cook for another 20 seconds. Whisk in the flour and stir that shit up so there aren't any dry clumps. Whisk in the white wine and the broth slowly so that you don't get any big chunks. Add the beans and let this simmer away for about 10 minutes, stirring this shit every couple of minutes, until it starts to thicken up. It should coat your spoon and basically start to look like pot pie filling. Add the lemon juice and fresh herbs and remove from the heat. Taste that shit and add more herbs, lemon juice, or salt based on what you're craving. You should get about 4 cups of filling.

(continued)

3 To assemble the pot pies, roll out the crust to about ¼ inch thick and cut it into a round (or rounds) so it fits on the top of your pie pan or ramekins. Pour the filling into your pie pan or ramekins, grease the edge, and lay the pie crust over the filling. Use a small knife to cut a couple vents in there to let out the steam as this fucker bakes.

4 Brush the crust with a little olive oil, place the pan or ramekins on the baking sheet, and throw it in the oven until the crust looks done, 20 to 30 minutes.

5 Let this cool for a couple minutes before serving because this comes out of the oven hotter than uptown funk.

* Feel free to drink the rest SLOWLY while you cook yourself something nice. You deserve that shit. No wine for you? Just add ½ cup vegetable broth to the pot instead.

** One 15-ounce can of beans, drained and rinsed, will work just fine.

*** You can do 2 tablespoons chives and no parsley or all parsley and no chives. Use whatever the fuck you've got.

TEMPEH AND SPINACH CALZONES
WITH ALMOND RICOTTA

MAKES 8 HAND-SIZE CALZONES, ENOUGH FOR 4 TO 8 PEOPLE DEPENDING ON YOUR SIDE SITUATION

These OG hot pockets are filling as hell and pack plenty of protein and greens in every bite. Serve them up with some Stuffed Mushrooms (page 55) and Big-Ass Salad Bowl (page 91) with Italian dressing (page 82) and you've got yourself an enviable spread.

Everyday Pizza Dough (page 226)

FILLING

2 teaspoons olive oil

8 ounces tempeh*

1 yellow onion, chopped

1 tablespoon soy sauce, tamari, or Bragg's*

2 teaspoons chopped fennel seeds**

1 teaspoon dried basil

1 teaspoon dried oregano

1 teaspoon dried thyme

6 cups spinach

1 tablespoon lemon juice

3 cloves garlic, minced

Red pepper flakes

ALMOND RICOTTA

⅓ cup sliced almonds, toasted***

14 ounces extra-firm tofu, drained

2 cloves garlic, minced

1 tablespoon olive oil

1 tablespoon lemon juice

½ teaspoon salt

⅓ cup nooch*

Spray oil

Quick Blender Marinara (page 162) or Blender Red Sauce (page 107), for dipping

1 Make the dough according to the directions on page 226 because we're not about to type that shit out again. Let it rise in one big ball and about 30 minutes before it's ready, start making the filling. If you made the dough ahead of time and stuck that shit in the fridge, just pull it out to warm up as you start the filling.

2 Warm your oven up 475°F. Set aside a large baking sheet.

3 Make the filling: Grab a large skillet or wok and warm up the olive oil over medium heat. Using your hands, crumble in the tempeh in pieces no bigger than a nickel. Smaller is way better than big-ass chunks. Add the onion and sauté them together until the tempeh starts to brown, about 5 minutes. Sprinkle the soy sauce all over the pan, stir, then add the fennel seeds, dried basil, oregano, and thyme. Sauté for 30 seconds, then fold in the spinach, lemon juice, and garlic. If that pan starts looking a little dry, add a couple tablespoons of water to loosen that shit up instead of pouring in a fuck-ton of added oil. Cook it up until the spinach is all wilted, about 2 more minutes. Turn off the heat and shake in some pepper flakes if you know you like that shit.

(continued)

4 Make the almond ricotta: Throw the almonds, tofu, garlic, olive oil, lemon juice, salt, and nooch together in a food processor or blender and run that shit until the almonds are in tiny-ass pieces and all mixed up. No food processor? Just chop the almonds up into tiny pieces and mash the tofu up with your hands. Mix in everything and you are good to go. No fucking excuses.

5 If you want the calzones to look extra fancy, you can layer the almond ricotta and the spinach/tempeh filling separately in the calzones. But if you could give 2 shits about that, mix the ricotta into the pan of spinach/tempeh filling now and stir that shit until it's all together.

6 Now assemble the goddamn things. Punch down the dough to let out all the gas (stop laughing) and knead it once or twice until it comes together into a ball. Cut that shit into 8 equal pieces. Grab one, and roll it, on a well-floured surface, into a vaguely round shape about ¼ inch thick. Pile on about ½ cup of the filling on one half of the round. (If you kept the fillings separate, spoon in about 2 tablespoons of tempeh and ⅓ cup ricotta.) Wet all around the edge with a little water to help that fucker stick shut. Pull the dough over to form a half-moon and press down the edge to close it up. You can kinda roll the edge up a little and press down or press down with a fork to make a legit crimp around the edge. Repeat to make 8 calzones.

7 Cut 2 or 3 little vents on top of the calzones with a small knife and put the finished calzones on the baking sheet. Spray the tops with a little oil and bake those fuckers until they are nice and golden, 15 to 20 minutes.

8 Serve warm with some dipping sauce.

* WTF? See page 231.

** Fennel seeds will be with all the other spices in the store. Or ½ teaspoon ground fennel is legit, too. Fennel helps add a badass Italian sausage kinda flavor to the dish, but if you don't want to buy a new spice that you'll never fucking use again, just leave it out.

*** Need help getting toasted? See page 218.

CURRY HAND PIES
WITH CILANTRO-MINT SAUCE

MAKES ABOUT
16 PIES (DEPENDING
ON THE SIZE YOU
CUT THAT SHIT)

These fuckers are flakey but in the best way possible. Stuffed to the brim with protein and spices, these are a worthy new edition to your culinary cache.

---

1 Make the filling: Grab a large skillet or wok and heat up the oil over medium heat. Add the onion and carrots and sauté until they start to get a little golden, 5 to 7 minutes. Add the split peas and green peas (no need to thaw the green peas, just throw those fuckers in frozen) and stir it up. Now add the curry powder, cumin, coriander, and cayenne and sauté for about 30 seconds or until your kitchen smells like a goddamn restaurant. Throw in the spinach, garlic, ginger, and soy sauce or tamari and keep cooking until the spinach starts wilting, about 2 minutes. Add the lemon juice and remove from the heat.

2 Now it's time to make the dough: In a large bowl, whisk together the flours, baking powder, curry powder, and salt. Make a well in the center of that and pour in the coconut milk. Stir that all together until everything is combined into a shaggy dough. If you need more liquid add a tablespoon or two of coconut milk to fix that shit, up to ¼ cup. Shape it up into a nice ball. You can make the dough the night before and just stick it in the fridge in a plastic bag. That's day-old dough in the photo on page 151. #realtalk

3 Now, to make some fucking pies. Heat your oven up to 375°F. Line a large baking sheet with parchment paper or foil.

FILLING

2 teaspoons olive, grapeseed, or coconut oil

½ yellow onion, chopped (the size of peas)

2 carrots, chopped (the size of peas)

2 cups cooked yellow split peas*

1 cup frozen green peas

½ teaspoon of your favorite no-salt curry powder

¼ teaspoon ground cumin

¼ teaspoon ground coriander**

⅛ teaspoon cayenne pepper

2 cups spinach, cut into thin strips

2 cloves garlic, minced

2 teaspoons minced fresh ginger

1 tablespoon soy sauce or tamari

1 tablespoon lemon or lime juice

(continued)

DOUGH

1¼ cups whole wheat pastry flour***

1 cup all-purpose flour***

1 tablespoon baking powder

1 tablespoon of your favorite no-salt curry powder

½ teaspoon salt

1 cup canned coconut milk

Spray oi!

SAUCE

1½-inch piece of fresh ginger, peeled****

1 jalapeño, seeded and chopped

2 cups fresh mint leaves*****

2 cups cilantro*****

¼ cup lemon juice

¼ cup water

½ teaspoon salt

4 Cut the ball of dough in half and throw half of it onto a well-floured surface. Roll it out into an oval shape about ⅛ inch thick. Now grab a biscuit cutter, bowl, or mug about twice the size you want your pies and cut out a bunch of rounds. We like to use a 3½-inch bowl, but you do you. Cover about half of one round with a good amount of filling and leave about a finger's width around the edge, cause, you know you've got to close that shit. Wet your fingers (with water, not spit, unless you are fucking disgusting) and run them around the edge to help them stick shut. Fold the dough over the filling, taco style, so you have a tasty as fuck half-moon. Press down the edge with your finger to seal it or use a fork so that you get those crimpy lines that people fucking love. Put the hand pie on the baking sheet and cut two or three tiny slits in the top as vents. Keep making pies until you run out of dough or filling.

5 Spray the tops with a little oil and pop them in the oven. Bake for 20 to 25 minutes, until the edges and bottoms start to look a little brown (we know that the yellow color of the dough makes that shit a little difficult, but just look closer).

6 While the pies are baking, make the sauce: Throw the ginger, jalapeño, mint, cilantro, lemon juice, water, and salt together in a blender or food processor and run that shit until a kind of paste/sauce hybrid comes together. Add a little more water if you want it saucier. Done.

7 Serve the sauce along with the hot hand pies. People will ask you where the fuck you order them from. Trust.

* No clue how to cook these sunshiny fuckers? See Basic Pot of Beans, page 211.

** Can't find it/don't want to fucking buy coriander? Just use more cumin instead.

*** You can use all whole wheat or all-purpose if that's all you've got. Not a big deal.

**** Don't go measuring this shit, just start with a piece of ginger that is about the same size and thickness as your thumb. If you know that you've got a big-ass thumb, size down.

***** Throwing in a bunch of mint stems will make this sauce bitter as hell so take a minute to pull off all the leaves one by one. Cilantro stems taste just like the leaves, so you can be reckless as fuck while measuring this shit out. Stems and leaves, whatever. Cilantro is chill like that.

FUCK DISHES
EAT WITH YOUR HANDS

CHEAT ON
PIZZA

CHERRY TOMATO GALETTES

Galette is just a fancy-ass term for a freeform pie, so don't let that word stop you from trying this. It's basically pizza's sister who spent a summer abroad. Sure it comes off a little snobby, but it's totally DTF: damn tasty food.

Olive Oil Crust (page 225)

FILLING
2 teaspoons olive oil

1 yellow onion, sliced

3 cups halved cherry tomatoes

¼ teaspoon salt

2 cloves garlic, minced

1 tablespoon balsamic vinegar

2 tablespoons chopped fresh basil, plus more for garnish

Olive oil, for brushing the crusts

1 Make the pie crust on page 225 through step 2. Let it chill out in the fridge while you make the filling. Also, crank your oven to 425°F.

2 Make the filling: Grab a large skillet or wok and heat up the oil over medium heat. Add the onions and sauté them around until those fuckers start to look a little golden, 5 to 7 minutes. Throw in the tomatoes and salt and keep sautéing until the tomatoes start breaking down a little bit, about 3 minutes. Add the garlic and balsamic and cook for a minute or two more, until most of the vinegar has evaporated. Once that shit is done, remove from the heat and stir in the basil. Taste and see if you need more salt or garlic. You know how you like shit.

3 To assemble the tart, roll out one of the crusts on a well-floured surface like your counter or a table until it's about ¼ inch thick. You want it kinda round, but that shit shouldn't be perfect; we're going for homemade as hell. Pile half the filling into the center of the crust leaving a 2-inch border around the edge. Fold the 2-inch border up and over the filling, brush the dough with some olive oil, and transfer it to a baking sheet. Do the same shit again with the other crust.

4 Bake until the crusts are looking nice and golden, 25 to 35 minutes. They should smell fucking amazing, but you need to wait a few minutes before you cut them up because those tiny-ass tomatoes are straight-up lava temperatures. Serve warm with some extra basil sprinkled over to really class that shit up.

BLACK-BEAN-AND-PUMPKIN MEXICAN LASAGNA

ENCHILADA-ISH SAUCE

1½ cups vegetable broth

1½ cups plain tomato sauce*

2 cloves garlic, minced

3 tablespoons mild chili powder

2 tablespoons lime juice

1 tablespoon soy sauce or tamari

½ teaspoon ground cumin

½ teaspoon dried oregano

Somewhere between enchiladas and lasagna you have this dish. And honestly, that's kinda the warmest and tastiest place we could imagine being.

1 First, make the enchilada-ish sauce: Pour everything together in a medium saucepan and bring it to a gentle simmer—not a boil, a goddamn simmer—and cook for about 15 minutes to give the sauce a chance to thicken up a little. Turn off the heat and get making the filling. You should have about 2½ cups.

2 Make the filling: In a large skillet or wok, heat the olive oil over medium heat. Add the onion and sauté until it starts to get golden, about 5 minutes. Add the bell pepper and keep cooking for about 2 minutes. Add the garlic, jalapeño, black beans, and corn. Stir that all up and let everything in the pan warm back up, about 2 minutes. Add the chili powder, cumin, smoked paprika, and salt and keep cooking until the spices get all warm and start making your kitchen smell legit, about 1 minute. Fold in the pumpkin, lime juice, and maple syrup and cook for another minute so the pumpkin gets mixed up and warm. Turn off the heat.

3 Heat up your oven to 375°F. Grab an 9 x 13-inch baking dish.

4 Now it's time to assemble this shit. Pour about ¾ cup of the enchilada-ish sauce all over the bottom of the baking dish. Cover that up with a single layer of tortillas. Yeah there will be some holes but just do your fucking best. Smear on a layer of the filling and try to keep that shit at an even thickness so you don't have a lopsided dish. Cover that with another layer of tortillas and ½ cup sauce. Repeat. Cover with the remaining sauce.

5 Cover that shit in foil and bake for 15 minutes. Uncover it and bake for 10 more.

6 Serve warm with some salsa and avocado on the side.

* Not marinara, just canned, no-seasoning tomato sauce. Simple shit. Grab a low-sodium one if you can find it.

** You can use two 15-ounces cans of beans, drained and rinsed, because we know you are about the dump-and-stir life.

*** Don't accidently grab pumpkin pie filling at the store and think that shit will still work because it fucking won't.

FILLING

2 teaspoons olive oil

1 medium yellow onion, chopped (the size of black beans)

1 red bell pepper, chopped (the size of black beans)

3 cloves garlic, minced

1 jalapeño, minced

3 cups cooked black beans**

1 cup fresh or frozen corn kernels

1½ teaspoons chili powder

½ teaspoon ground cumin

½ teaspoon smoked paprika

½ teaspoon salt

1½ cups canned pumpkin puree***

1 tablespoon lime juice

2 teaspoons maple syrup or agave syrup

12 flour tortillas or whatever you usually buy for burritos

Salsa (any of the shit from our first book would be legit)

Avocado

FILL UP ON PASTA
UNPLUG THE WIFI
GET HOUSEWIFE-WASTED

FAMILY-STYLE ROASTED VEGGIE PASTA

This pasta has been our party staple for fucking years. Wait till summer when all the produce is cheap and you'll be able to stretch this meal real far. And we promise, you'll be surprised by how all these average ingredients make for one badass bowl.

1 pound pasta*

1 tablespoon olive oil, plus more if needed for the pasta

½ large red onion, sliced

2 medium carrots, cut into thin matchsticks

1 pint tiny tomatoes, halved**

1 medium zucchini, cut into thin matchsticks

1 pound eggplant, skin on, cut into cubes

¼ teaspoon salt

2½ tablespoons chopped fresh thyme leaves

3 cloves garlic, minced

2 tablespoons lemon juice

3 tablespoons balsamic vinegar

½ teaspoon red pepper flakes (optional)***

Salt and black pepper

Serving ideas: fresh arugula or spinach leaves

We like penne or ziti, but use whateverthefuck you have.

*** If the tomatoes are really fucking tiny, like smaller than a marble, just leave 'em whole.*

*** Optional if you know that your shit is weak.*

1 Cook the pasta according to the package directions. We aren't going to waste our damn time typing that shit out. We already know you can read. Drain that shit and pour it back into the pot.

2 Crank up the oven to 425°F. Grab 2 large rimmed baking sheets.

3 In a large bowl, throw in the oil, red onion, carrots, tomatoes, zucchini, eggplant, and salt. Mix that shit up until everything looks coated. Spread it out on the baking sheets and then slip them in the oven.

4 Roast for 20 minutes, then take them out, add the thyme, garlic, and lemon juice, stir, and throw them back in the oven until some of the veggies start looking a little browned around the edges, 10 to 15 minutes longer. A few burned pieces aren't going to hurt anybody, so calm the fuck down.

5 Add the roasted veggies to the cooked pasta, pour in the balsamic, pepper flakes, a pinch of salt and black pepper, and stir that shit up. If the pasta looks a little dry add a tablespoon of olive oil to lube it all up. Taste and add more garlic, vinegar, lemon juice, thyme, whateverthefuck you like. If you want to up the greens level, serve the hot pasta on a bed of arugula or spinach with a squeeze of lemon juice on them. Done and done.

BAKED ZITI WITH SPINACH

1 can (14 ounces) water-packed artichoke hearts, drained and rinsed

12 ounces firm silken tofu, drained

¼ cup sliced almonds

3 tablespoons nooch*

2 tablespoons lemon juice

3 cloves garlic, 2 whole and 1 minced

¼ teaspoon salt

2 teaspoons olive oil

½ yellow onion, chopped

4 cups chopped spinach

Squeeze of lemon juice

Pinch of salt

¼ cup chopped fresh basil

1 pound pasta,** cooked according to the package it fucking came in

3 cups Quick Blender Marinara (page 162) or Blender Red Sauce (page 107)

TOPPING
3 tablespoons bread crumbs

1 tablespoon nooch*

¼ teaspoon garlic powder

1 tablespoon olive oil

This ziti is so goddamn good it doesn't even need a photo. Like, what is that photo over there on the next page? It doesn't have jack shit to do with this recipe. THAT'S just how fucking good this pasta is. No hype, all delivery.

---

1 Warm up your oven to 350°F. Have an 8 x 10-inch baking dish handy.

2 In a blender or food processor, combine the artichoke hearts, tofu, almonds, nooch, lemon juice, whole cloves of garlic, and salt and run until there aren't any big chunks. (You have a shitty blender that was just never the same after that one party? Just add a tablespoon of water to help get that shit going as you bang on the side. #beenthere)

3 In a medium skillet, heat the oil up over medium heat. Add the onion and sauté until it starts to look kinda see-thru, about 3 minutes. Add the spinach, minced garlic, lemon juice, and salt and sauté until the spinach has wilted and given up that leaf life, about 3 minutes. Turn off the heat.

4 In a big bowl, mix together the tofu-artichoke mixture, spinach-onion mixture, basil, and cooked pasta until there aren't any big globs in there.

5 Grab the baking dish and cover the bottom with 1 cup of the marinara. Pour in the pasta mixture in an even layer, then pour the rest of the marinara over the top and kinda smear it around with the back of a spoon so that all the pasta gets coated.

6 Make the topping: In a small bowl, mix together the bread crumbs, nooch, and garlic powder. In a small skillet, heat up the oil over medium heat. Add the bread crumb mixture and sauté until everything is coated in oil and it smells kinda toasty, about 3 minutes.

7 Sprinkle the bread crumbs over the top of the pasta, cover it with foil, and stick it in the oven for 25 minutes. After 25 minutes, take off the foil, and bake it uncovered for 10 minutes longer. Let that shit cool for a couple of minutes before serving.

* WTF? See page 231.

** You know, like ziti or some other tube-like shit.

MEATBALL SUBS

Go ahead and get all the "ball" jokes outta your system now. You're an adult. Who pays bills. So just get the giggles out and we'll wait. You good? Alright, let's roll some balls with our hands.

---

1 Crank your oven to 400°F. Spray a baking sheet with oil.

2 Mash up the beans and lentils in a large bowl until they form a paste. Some whole bean bits are cool, but try to keep that shit to a minimum. Stir in the rest of the ingredients for the balls and mix it all up so that everything gets distributed. You might need to use your hands because it's just the best fucking way to do this with a quickness. You can use a spoon if you want, but we'll be silently judging you. If the stuff you are mixing up feels a little dry, add a tablespoon or two of water.

3 Roll the mixture into balls about the size of a golf ball and put them on the baking sheet. You should get 20 to 25 depending on your rolling skills. Coat them lightly with oil and bake, turning them over halfway, until both sides are golden brown, about 30 minutes.

4 While the balls are cooking, make the marinara. The sauce is gonna keep our balls nice and moist.

5 When the balls are almost ready to go, throw the sauce into a medium saucepan and warm it up over medium heat. Cut your rolls or bread in half and throw them in the oven with the balls to warm up for a minute.

6 When all that shit is ready, assemble your subs. Spoon a little marinara on the bottom half of the bread, put 3 or 4 meatballs on

(continued)

BEAN BALLS
Spray oil

1½ cups cooked kidney beans*

1½ cups cooked brown lentils**

¼ cup chopped onion***

⅓ cup whole wheat bread crumbs

3 cloves garlic, minced

¼ cup nooch**** or flour

2 tablespoons olive oil

1 tablespoon soy sauce or tamari

2 teaspoons no-salt, all-purpose seasoning blend

½ teaspoon dried oregano

½ teaspoon dried thyme

½ teaspoon grated lemon zest*****

Quick Blender Marinara (page 162)

6 crusty sub-style rolls; or 2 baguettes cut into 6 sandwich-size lengths

Arugula, for serving

top, lather those bastards in marinara sauce to your liking, add a handful of arugula for color, then top it off with the other half of the bread. Get it down immediately or someone is going to eat that fucker for you.

* Or one 15-ounce can of beans, drained and rinsed.

** No clue how to do this shit? See Basic Pot of Beans, page 211.

*** White, yellow, or sweet onion will do. Whatever is on sale.

**** WTF? See page 231.

***** No clue how to zest? See page 218.

QUICK BLENDER MARINARA

MAKES ABOUT 6½ CUPS

5 cloves garlic

1 tablespoon olive oil

1½ teaspoons dried thyme

½ teaspoon dried oregano

Pinch of red pepper flakes

2 cans (28 ounces each) whole tomatoes*

Pinch of salt

In a blender or food processor, throw in the garlic, olive oil, thyme, oregano, pepper flakes, and salt and pulse until that shit is all minced up. Grab the cans of tomatoes and drain off the extra liquid. (But save the liquid you drained off and use it in your next soup or to thin out some pasta sauce. WASTE NOT, WANT NOT, MOTHERFUCKER.) Dump the canned tomatoes right into the blender. Run that fucker until the tomatoes are nice and broken down. Done. Just stick it in the fridge or freeze for later.

* Make sure there isn't a shit-ton of salt or any other seasoning in those tomatoes.

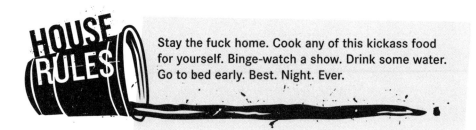

HOUSE RULES

Stay the fuck home. Cook any of this kickass food for yourself. Binge-watch a show. Drink some water. Go to bed early. Best. Night. Ever.

CREAMY WHITE BEAN AND ARUGULA SANDWICHES

Been avoiding salads for a while, like for years now? Well get your ass halfway there with this refreshing motherfucker. Both filling and full of greens, this is a sammie you can feel good about. Fuck it, just imagine the bread counts as croutons. You basically just ate a salad. Boom.

3 cups cooked white or cannellini beans*

1 avocado

3 tablespoons lemon juice

½ red onion, chopped

½ cup chopped cucumber (about ½ cucumber)

¼ cup chopped fresh basil

2 cloves garlic, minced

½ teaspoon cayenne pepper (optional)**

Salt

4 cups arugula

1 tablespoon olive oil

12 slices crusty bread, toasted because you know how to live

1 large tomato, sliced

1 Grab a big bowl and throw in the beans, avocado, and lemon juice and mash the fuck out of the whole thing. Some chunks are fine, but you're looking for a 60-40 ratio of bean paste to bean chunks. Fold in the onion, cucumber, basil, garlic, cayenne (if using), and ½ teaspoon salt and mix it all together.

2 In a separate bowl toss together the arugula, oil, and a pinch of salt.

3 Now assemble the sammies. Throw a handful of the arugula mix down on the bread, pile on a bunch of the white bean mixture, then top it with a couple tomato slices. Press the other piece of bread down on top, you know, like a fucking sandwich. Then eat it, like a fucking sandwich.

* Or two 15-ounce cans of beans, drained and rinsed, if you're making this shit on the go.

** Optional, but consider yourself fucking peer-pressured.

MAKES ENOUGH
FOR 6 FULL-SIZE
SANDWICHES OR
12 HALF SANDWICHES
BECAUSE, YOU
KNOW, MATH

ROASTED CAULIFLOWER AND MUSHROOM BANH MI

ROASTED MARINATED VEGETABLES

2 tablespoons soy sauce or tamari

3 tablespoons rice vinegar

1 tablespoon lime juice

1 tablespoon neutral oil, such as grapeseed

2 teaspoons brown sugar

1 teaspoon Sriracha-style hot sauce

3 cups bite-size cauliflower florets*

2 medium shiitake mushrooms, stems discarded, caps sliced into strips**

½ cup panko bread crumbs***

2 teaspoons yellow no-salt added curry powder

¾ cup chopped shallots or onion

1 tablespoon minced fresh ginger

This is hands down one of our favorite fucking recipes. Far from traditional, our version of this Vietnamese sandwich is filled with cauliflower and mushrooms because we do our own thing. And you should too. BE YOURSELF AND EAT A FUCKING SANDWICH.

1 Prepare the vegetables: In a large bowl, mix together the soy sauce or tamari, vinegar, lime juice, oil, sugar, and hot sauce. Add the cauliflower and mushrooms and let them sit for about 15 minutes but no longer than 2 hours. When you're ready to get going, start warming up the oven to 400°F and grab a baking sheet.

2 In a medium bowl, mix together the panko and the curry powder. Drain the cauliflower and mushrooms then toss those fibrous bastards in the panko mix along with the shallots and ginger. Mix that all up until everything looks coated and pour it out onto the baking sheet. Roast, stirring it up halfway, until the cauliflower is starting to look nice and crispy, about 25 minutes.

3 While the cauliflower mixture is roasting you have time to get the rest of the shit together. Don't look at your phone; that shit will only distract you and you're on sandwich duty. To make the slaw: Just throw the radishes, carrots, vinegar, soy sauce or tamari, lime juice, and agave together in a bowl and toss it. So. Fucking. Simple.

4 Make the aioli if you are using it and get the rest of your toppings in order. You got this shit.

5 When the vegetables are all roasted and looking right, spread your sammie-size baguette pieces with some aioli and fill up with slaw, cilantro, and all the rest of the toppers. Pile the roasted vegetables high inside the bread and keep making sammies until you run out of bread. Serve hot or at room temp. These badasses taste great no matter what the fuck you do. Serve these the day you make them though, so that the panko stays crispy and delicious. You're fucking welcome.

* You'll need about 1 small crown cauliflower. And florets are just little-ass trees, don't freak the fuck out.

** You should get about 1½ cups sliced mushrooms. Can't find shiitakes? Just do button instead, but try to keep the strips from being too thick because that will not be nearly as fucking tasty.

*** WTF is that? See page 231.

RADISH AND CARROT SLAW

4 medium radishes, cut into matchsticks (about 1 cup)

2 medium carrots, cut into matchsticks (about 1 cup)

3 tablespoons rice vinegar

1 teaspoon soy sauce or tamari

1 tablespoon lime juice

1 teaspoon agave syrup or your favorite liquid sweetener

Sriracha Aioli (optional; page 107)

2 crusty baguettes, each cut into 3 sammie-size lengths and sliced in half

Optional toppers: cilantro, mint, cucumber rounds, jalapeño slices

FEAST FROM THE EAST

This is a must-do menu when it's hot as fuck outside and you just wanna stuff your face with some tasty grub that won't leave you sweating through your shirt. Take down the takeout menu from your fridge because you're done with that sodium-laced shit. Also, practice your chopstick skills because that shit is embarrassing.

» **PAD THAI ROLLS** (page 40) or **BAKED SPRING ROLLS** (page 57)

» **CALIFORNIA CITRUS AND ALMOND SALAD** (page 97)

» **SCRAMBLED CURRY TOFU FRIED RICE** (page 32)

» **ROASTED CAULIFLOWER AND MUSHROOM BANH MI** (page 164)

» **HIGH SCHOOL–STYLE HARD LEMONADE** (page 198)

QUESO-ISH QUESADILLAS

We like to make a double batch of Butternut Squash Queso-ish Dip (page 46) for a party and then throw together these motherfuckers too. Everybody loves quesadillas and these are so goddamn good that there's no way you'll get stuck with dish duty. Serve with a side of your favorite salsa and some Everyday Guacamole (page 67).

2 teaspoons olive oil

1 red bell pepper, chopped

½ cup corn kernels*

1½ cups cooked pinto beans**

¼ teaspoon ground cumin

Pinch of salt

1 cup Butternut Squash Queso-ish Dip (page 46)

2 cups shredded cabbage, red or green

6 burrito-size tortillas, whatever kind you like

Frozen corn is okay to use. It's not the star of the fucking show in this recipe.

** *One 15-ounce can of beans is totally fine, but drain and rinse those fuckers.*

*** *You don't know how badly we just wanted to write "Now throw that fucker in a quesadilla, just figure it out." Explaining how to construct a quesadilla feels like explaining how to breathe.*

1 In a medium skillet or sauté pan, warm up the olive oil over medium heat. Add the bell pepper and corn and sauté for 2 minutes so that bell pepper starts getting a little soft. Add the pinto beans and do your best to smash a good amount of those fibrous motherfuckers up so that you get a little paste going in some spots. Throw in the cumin and salt and sauté for another 30 seconds. It should smell dope as hell. Pour in ¾ cup of the butternut queso and stir until everything is all mixed up and warm, 1 to 2 minutes depending on if you had your queso in the fridge or whatever. Fold in the cabbage and turn off the heat.

2 To make a quesadilla***, grab your griddle or large flat-bottomed pan and warm the fucker up over medium heat. Throw on a tortilla and warm up both sides for about 15 seconds. Still on the griddle, spread 3 or 4 spoonfuls of the filling over half the tortilla so that it's no more than a ½ inch thick. Spread on a little of the remaining queso and fold the tortilla over so you are left with a delicious-as-hell half-moon. Flip it over on the griddle for another 20 seconds so both sides are nice and crispy and then take it off. Repeat all this until you are out of filling, queso, and tortillas.

3 Cut the quesadillas into little pizza-shaped wedges and serve warm. Make sure you save yourself one, because these fuckers will go fast.

DESSERTS, DRINKS, AND SIDES OF SWEETNESS

DON'T FUCK AROUND WITH
SWEETS SCARIER THAN
YOUR MOVIE SELECTION

ROSEMARY CARAMEL CORN

MAKES ENOUGH
FOR 6 TO 8 PEOPLE
TO MUNCH ON

You might be thinking it's unnatural to combine rosemary and caramel corn, but that shit works. Unlikely combinations have given us such amazing things as *Alien vs. Predator*, plumcots, and *Bananas in Pyjamas*. Keep an open mind and taste the future of dessert. Oh yeah.

8 cups unseasoned popped popcorn*

¼ cup refined coconut oil

1 tablespoon loosely packed chopped fresh rosemary

⅓ cup packed brown sugar

¼ cup maple syrup

½ teaspoon salt

½ teaspoon baking soda

1 Warm up your oven to 250°F. Line a rimmed baking sheet with parchment paper.

2 Pour the popcorn in one big bowl with tall sides or two medium bowls so that you don't spill it later while you're trying to mix.

3 In a small saucepan, melt the coconut oil over medium heat. When it's totally clear, add the rosemary and stir around for about 30 seconds. Add the brown sugar, maple syrup, and salt and simmer that shit for 2½ to 3 minutes, stirring constantly so nothing burns. You want the sugar crystals to dissolve and a nice constant roll of bubbles through the whole sauce.

4 Stir in the baking soda and remove from the heat. It will kinda bubble up and turn less see-thru. Don't worry. Mix it up well and pour it over the popcorn. Stir and stir until all that shit is lightly coated in that kick-ass caramel. Don't taste it yet because you will burn the shit out of your tongue.

5 Pour the popcorn on the lined baking sheet in an even layer. Turn off the heat for the oven and then throw the baking sheet in. Leave it in there for 15 minutes to harden up and then serve. Store it in an airtight container or bag, but don't plan on leftovers if you've got a full house.

* Save some damn money and pop this yourself. See page 220 for how to do it on your stovetop for almost nothing.

OAT TOPPING
¾ cup oat flour*

¼ cup packed brown sugar

1 teaspoon ground cinnamon

½ teaspoon ground ginger

3 tablespoons olive or grapeseed oil

CAKE
1 cup unsweetened plain nondairy milk

1 teaspoon lemon juice or apple cider vinegar

1 tablespoon loosely packed grated lemon zest**

⅓ cup granulated sugar

¼ cup olive or grapeseed oil

1 teaspoon vanilla extract

1¼ cups whole wheat pastry or all-purpose flour

½ cup oat flour*

2½ teaspoons baking powder

½ teaspoon salt

2 cups fresh or frozen blackberries

BLACKBERRY-LEMON BUCKLE

A buckle is like a coffee cake except with a ton of fucking fruit that makes the cake "buckle" because it's so heavy. It might not be the prettiest cake on the block, but come summer with all those delicious berries popping up it's the only shit we make when we've got to bring dessert someplace. Blueberries and raspberries are legit as hell in here too if that's what's looking best when you're at the market.

---

1 Heat up the oven to 375°F. Grease and flour a 9-inch springform cake or deep-dish pie pan. Don't be lazy from the jump, do this shit.

2 First make the oat topping: Mix the flour, brown sugar, and spices in a medium bowl. Drizzle in the oil and crumble it around with your fingers so that you get little pea-size bits of oil all through that shit. Done.

3 Now for the badass cake batter: In a glass, add the lemon juice to the milk and set it aside for a few minutes.

4 In a large bowl, mix together the lemon zest, granulated sugar, oil, and vanilla. In a smaller bowl, whisk together the flours, baking powder, and salt.

5 Add the milk mixture to the bowl with the sugar and stir that shit up. Now, slowly stir the flour mixture into the bowl with all the wet stuff. Mix them all together until everything is well combined. The batter will be thick as hell, but you're all good so keep going. Fold in 1½ cups of the berries and stir a few times to make sure they are mixed in.

(continued)

6 Now we assemble this tasty son of a bitch. Pour the batter into the prepared pan and then throw the remaining berries on top. Gently press those plump bastards into the batter a little bit so they aren't like loose and shit all over that cake. Just a gentle pat will be all good. Evenly sprinkle the oat topping over all of that and throw the pan in the oven on the middle rack. Bake until the topping appears golden and a toothpick stuck into the center comes out without a bunch of raw batter all desperate and clinging to it, 35 to 45 minutes .

7 Let the cake cool for at least 45 minutes to 1 hour in the pan before serving since those berries are crazy fucking hot on the inside. You can make this shit the day before if you have stronger willpower than us and won't dig into as soon as that fucker is done.

* Oat flour might sound fancy, but it's really fucking not. Just measure out some rolled oats, throw them in a blender or food processor, and run it until that shit looks like flour. Done.

** No clue how to zest? See page 218.

HOUSE RULES

Cut your dessert up into reasonable slices before you set it out to keep a greedy motherfucker from eating half a pie and blaming you. (Dogs don't respect the slice system though.)

CHOCOLATE-ALMOND HAYSTACKS

Swear you can't bake without burning something? No stress. We're confident in your melting skills, and that's all you need to do for these simple sons of bitches. They look so good that no one will know exactly how little work you actually fucking did.

1½ cups semisweet chocolate chips

2 teaspoons unrefined coconut oil*

2 cups sliced almonds, toasted**

½ teaspoon sea salt***

1 Line a rimmed baking sheet with some parchment or wax paper.

2 Melt the chocolate chips in a double boiler, homemade fake-out, or the microwave (see page 218). Add the coconut oil to the chocolate chips and stir until everything is melted and mixed together. Remove from the heat.

3 Add the almonds to the melted chocolate and stir that shit up until there's no more dry clumps of almonds. This is the most work in the whole goddamn recipe: mixing.

4 Once everything is coated, grab a big spoon and dollop piles of the chocolate-almond mixture (about the size of an egg) onto the lined baking sheet. Sprinkle each haystack with some sea salt and then put the baking sheet in a cool area to let the chocolate harden up before diving in, 15 to 45 minutes depending on the temperature in your place. So maybe don't try this shit on a hot summer day. You can stick this in the fridge if you're in a rush and have the space.

* Unrefined coconut oil adds a great sorta buttery flavor to the chocolate. If you don't have it, refined is cool, too.

** Don't know how to toast nuts? See page 218.

*** We recommend a salt that is all big and fancy-looking, like large flaky crystals— whatever the best-looking salt you got will do. It's alright to be judgey with your salt's appearance. But any salt will do in a pinch.

FUDGY-AS-FUCK BROWNIES

¾ cup unsweetened milk, warm or at room temperature

2 tablespoons ground flax seeds

½ teaspoon apple cider vinegar or lemon juice

1¼ cups semisweet chocolate chips

3 tablespoons refined coconut oil

1 tablespoon neutral oil, like grapeseed

1 cup all-purpose or whole wheat pastry flour

½ cup unsweetened cocoa powder*

½ teaspoon baking soda

½ teaspoon salt

¾ cup sugar

1 tablespoon vanilla extract

If you like a slice of cake cut into the shape of a brownie, just move on because there's nothing for you here. Now if you like a brownie that tastes like a goddamn brownie and not a piece of chocolate cake, then a tray of this deliciousness is just right for you. If you're still reading, congratufuckinglations you have excellent taste.

1 Heat your oven up to 350°F. Line an 8-inch square pan with parchment paper with some popping over the edges so you can lift the brownies out later.

2 In a small glass, mix together the milk, ground flax seeds, and vinegar with a fork real well so there aren't any clumps. Set all that shit aside.

3 In a double boiler, homemade fake-out, or microwave, melt the chocolate chips and the oils together until they are all mixed up. Already confused? See page 218.

4 While that's all melting, grab a medium bowl and whisk together the flour, cocoa powder, baking soda, and salt.

5 When the chocolate and oil mixture is ready, remove it from the heat and stir in the sugar and vanilla really well. Now add the milk-flax mixture, a little at a time, until it's really fucking in there.

6 Now pour in the flour mixture and stir that shit up until it's just kinda mixed in and there aren't a ton of white parts. It's gonna be thick, but just trust us. The more you mix that shit up, the more likely it is your brownies are gonna get all sunk in the middle, so don't fuck this up.

7 Pour the mixture in the pan and kinda smear it around so it's all even. Bake until a toothpick stuck in the middle comes out mostly clean, 30 to 40 minutes. Take it out of the pan after 10 minutes and let it cool completely on a wire rack. If you dig in before it cools, then all that shit will just crumble on you. Be strong and just fucking wait 20 minutes.

8 Cut it up into whatever sizes you want and have at it. Store in the fridge.

You might see some shit at the store labeled "Dutch processed cocoa." Don't grab that one, it's different.

TAKE YOUR TASTE BUDS ON VACATION TO PIE-AMI

CHOCOLATE-COCONUT PIE

Sometimes all you need to get people to come together is a damn fine pie. This is that pie.

**MAKES ONE
9-INCH PIE**

½ batch Extra Flakey Coconut Oil Crust (page 224)

FILLING
½ cup semisweet chocolate chips

1 can (14 ounces) coconut milk, well chilled*

¼ cup powdered sugar

1 teaspoon vanilla extract

Pinch of salt

Whipped Cream (page 219)

1 Make the pie crust on page 224 through step 3. Let it chill out in the fridge while you make the filling. Also, start cranking your oven up to 400°F.

2 Follow the instructions on page 222 to roll out and blind bake the crust. Oh don't start whining about turning pages, you're getting a fucking pie out of this. While that cools, make the filling.

3 Make the filling: You need a handheld electric mixer or a stand mixer to do this shit. Stick the bowl and the beaters in the freezer for 15 minutes. This helps make sure that your mix won't turn into a puddle while you whip it.

4 While you're letting that do its thing, melt the chocolate chips in a double boiler or in the microwave. No fucking clue? See page 218. Let it cool slightly.

5 Take the shit out of the freezer and grab the coconut milk from the fridge without shaking it up. Open the can and scoop out all the thick white cream on the top half of the can and put it in the chilled bowl. You should have about 1 cup. (Leave that clearish liquid in the can and use it for something else later. A smoothie? A prank? We don't give a fuck. You don't need that shit now.)

(continued)

6 Sift the powdered sugar into the coconut cream so that there aren't any chunks. Add the vanilla. Now beat the hell out of it on medium-high. Slowly stream in the melted chocolate and the salt. Keep those beaters going until it starts looking all fluffy and delicious, about 2 minutes. Spread this all over the bottom of your pie crust in an even layer because that is the only way to do this shit.

7 Now make the whipped cream (yeah, it's almost like the same shit all over again) and spread that over the top. Let that fucker chill for at least 1 hour before serving. This pie holds up, so it's great to make the day before if you're on the ball like that and can plan shit out. Leftovers will keep for 3 to 4 days, but who the fuck has that kind of willpower?

* Put the coconut milk in the fridge the night before so you know it's cold enough.

HOUSE RULES

If you want to make this fucker look extra fancy, grab a bar of chocolate and shave some off using your veggie peeler, like you're peeling a carrot. It will look classy as hell and take you all of 1 minute. Plus, extra chocolate for you. No veggie peeler? Get your shit together.

PEAR AND POPPY SEED POUND CAKE

This is some high-tea shit right here. Serve this fucker alongside the Deviled Chickpea Bites (page 64) and the Melon and Mint Fruit Salad (page 5) for a classy time regardless of your mismatched plateware.

1 Warm up the oven to 350°F. Lightly grease a 9 x 5-inch loaf pan.

2 Throw the coconut oil and the sugar together in a medium bowl. Beat those fuckers together with an electric mixer on medium speed until it looks fluffy, almost frosting like. Beat in the yogurt, milk, and extracts until those guys are all mixed in. Add 1 cup of the flour, turn the mixer to low, and mix that fucker until they just start combining. Add the remaining 1 cup flour, the baking powder, poppy seeds, and cardamom and beat that sweet motherfucker again until everything just starts getting mixed up. Fold in the grated pear with a spatula and stir it around just enough that there isn't a giant pear colony somewhere in that batter.

3 Grab the loaf pan and pour that shit in, kinda smoothing out the top. Place on the middle rack of the oven and bake until the top looks golden and a toothpick stuck in it doesn't come out covered in raw batter, about 55 minutes. Let it cool in the pan for about 15 minutes, then pull it out and let it cool to room temperature on a wire rack.

4 Serve it just like this with some tea or spoonful of whipped cream if you're livin' it up like that.

¼ cup refined coconut oil, soft but not all melty

¾ cup sugar*

¾ cup plain nondairy yogurt

¼ cup unsweetened nondairy milk

1 teaspoon vanilla extract

1 teaspoon almond extract**

2 cups all-purpose or whole wheat pastry flour

2 teaspoons baking powder

2 teaspoons poppy seeds

¼ teaspoon ground cardamom***

1¼ cups grated pear (about 1 big one)

Yeah, it's a goddamn dessert. Calm down.

*** It's cool to skip the almond extract and use all vanilla if that is what you've got in your place.*

*** Cardamom is legit as hell and can be found in stuff like your favorite curries and chais. If your store doesn't carry it, they fucking suck. You can sub in cinnamon but def use cardamom if you can find it.*

½ batch Extra Flakey
Coconut Oil Crust
(page 224)

FILLING
3 cups fresh corn
kernels, cut right off the
cob*

½ cup unsweetened plain
almond or coconut milk

¼ cup brown sugar

2 teaspoons vanilla
extract

¼ teaspoon salt

Whipped Cream
(optional; page 219)

FRESH CORN BUTTER PIE

JUST HEAR US OUT. This isn't any weirder
than a pie made out of pumpkin if you
really fucking think about it. This is a
sweet and perfectly light custard that
comes together in a goddamn flash, so
don't be scared to try new shit.

1 Make the pie crust through step 3. Let it chill out in the fridge
while you make the filling. Also, start cranking your oven up to
425°F.

2 Make the filling: In a blender, throw the corn, milk, brown
sugar, vanilla, and salt all together and run that motherfucker for
a minute or two to get all the fiber from the corn to break down.
You shouldn't have to go for more than a minute and a half if you
have a decent blender. You know what kind of garbage shit you
are working with, not us.

3 On a well floured surface, roll out your pie dough and press it
into a 9-inch pie pan. Cut off any extra hanging over the edges
and press the edge of the crust into a pattern: Pinch it around
your pointer finger or make a pattern with a fork. Whatever.

4 Pour that filling right into the pie shell and stick it in the oven.
Immediately reduce the oven temperature to 375°F and bake that
fucker until the crust is golden and the center doesn't look all wet
and wobbly if you shake the pie a little, 35 to 45 minutes.

5 Let it cool for at least 1 hour before serving. This pie is great
kinda warmish but also tasty as hell if you let it chill overnight and
serve it cold. Top it with whipped cream if you want to get fancy.

*About 4 large ears of corn. The filling sets so much better if you use fresh corn
kernels. If it worked well with frozen, we promise we would tell you that shit.*

APPLE-COCONUT BUNDT CAKE

1 pound apples, peeled, cored, and cut into small cubes no larger than a dime (about 3 cups)*

2 tablespoons plus 3 cups whole wheat pastry or all-purpose flour

1 can (14 ounces) coconut milk, about 1½ cups

⅔ cup unsweetened plain milk

2 tablespoons grapeseed or olive oil

½ cup sugar

¼ cup packed brown sugar

2 teaspoons vanilla extract

1 tablespoon apple cider vinegar

2 teaspoons baking powder

1 teaspoon baking soda

½ teaspoon salt

2 teaspoons ground cinnamon

½ teaspoon ground ginger

⅛ teaspoon ground cloves or cardamom**

1 cup finely shredded unsweetened coconut

Powdered sugar and Whipped Cream (page 219), for serving

Why a Bundt cake? Because as every grandma knows, nothing says "I came over just to do some shit talkin'" better than a Bundt. So next time you want to get the crew together just to get some dirt, bring this sweet son of a bitch and you'll get the real good shit, like why Uncle Don is really missing that thumb.

1 Warm the oven to 325°F. Grease and flour a Bundt pan and set it aside.

2 In a large measuring cup, toss the cubed apples with 2 tablespoons of the flour until the apples are coated. Set that shit aside.

3 In a large bowl, stir together the milks, oil, sugars, extract, and vinegar. Mix well until all the ingredients are incorporated.

4 In a separate large bowl, whisk together the remaining 3 cups flour, the baking powder, baking soda, salt, and spices. Pour half the flour mixture into the milk mixture and stir that batter up until there are no more large dry spots. Add the second half and do the same shit. Once there are no more dry patches in the batter, gently fold in the apples and the coconut. The batter will be thick, but you haven't done anything wrong, so keep going. Pour the mixture into the prepared pan and kinda spread that shit around so it looks even. If you got fancy and picked up an extra detailed Bundt pan, let the mixture sit for a couple minutes so that the thick batter has time to settle into all the detailing.

5 Throw that shit onto the middle rack of the oven and bake until a toothpick stuck into multiple areas of the cake comes out clean, 45 minutes to 1 hour. You got to test around with a Bundt. Let the cake cool in the pan for 10 minutes. Then using a plate to cover the bottom of the pan, flip that shit over so that the cake it sitting on the plate. Let it cool completely while it chills out there.

6 Serve with a light dusting of powdered sugar and some whipped cream. (Or with a side of yogurt if you are calling this shit breakfast. This is a safe space. No judgment.)

* Whatever kind of crisp apples you like to eat will work here.

** This spice is fucking delicious, but if you don't want to hunt this shit down, just add the same amount of cinnamon.

HOUSE RULES

Want to talk shit but don't have a Bundt pan? Ninety-eight percent of thrift stores we've been in have at least one Bundt lying around. If you really can't find one, grab an angel food cake pan instead. This cake demands a hole in the center to replicate the shit-talking circle of the neighbor gossips, so come correct.

SAVOR SUMMER WITH THIS SWEET SNACK

BANANA AND COCONUT POPS

MAKES ABOUT
4½ CUPS FILLING,
ENOUGH FOR
10 POPS, BUT
THAT SHIT VARIES
BASED ON YOUR
MOLDS, HALVE THE
RECIPE IF YOUR
MOLDS ARE SMALL

These frozen motherfuckers come together in a sec with a blender and have all the best parts of banana bread without turning on the oven. Don't let summer slip by without making a tray of these.

6 ripe bananas

1 cup canned coconut milk

1½ cups nondairy yogurt*

3 tablespoons maple syrup or agave syrup

2 tablespoons orange juice

1 tablespoon ground cinnamon

2 teaspoons vanilla extract

1 Throw everything into a blender and give it a goddamn whirl until there are no chunks of banana left in there and everything looks smooth.

2 Pour this into your popsicle molds and stick in the freezer for about 40 minutes. If you don't have a mold with built-in sticks, after 40 minutes, take out your pop molds and then push popsicle sticks in. Freezing these fuckers a little bit first helps make sure you won't push the stick all the way through and end up with a slushie kebab that falls on the floor right away. Learn from our messy-ass mistakes. Please. If you have those fancy popsicle molds that stop this from happening, then congratufuckinglations.

3 Freeze until completely frozen. Yeah, we have to say that shit because people are impatient. Then kick back with one whenever life gets too hot to handle. They will keep for at least a month in the freezer.

We used coconut yogurt to keep that shit on theme, but use whatever you can find, like almond or soy. Just get plain or vanilla. None of that blueberry and banana bullshit. Use some damn sense.

PIÑA COLADA ICEES

2 cups ice cubes

1½ cups frozen pineapple chunks

1½ cups pineapple juice

¾ cup white rum*

½ cup canned coconut milk

2 bananas, broken into chunks and frozen

2 tablespoons agave syrup or your favorite liquid sweetener**

This piña colada has all the taste but half the fat of that bullshit you grab at the bar. The frozen banana makes it creamy as hell and keeps you from adding all that extra coconut milk so this baby goes down easy. Keep your freezer stocked with bananas because you just found your summer staple.

Throw everything in a blender that can fucking handle some ice and let that shit run until your drink as is smooth as you imagine yourself being after you drink it.

Or, you know, whatever amount of rum you want based on how shitty your day was. No judgment here. Not drinking? Substitute water or coconut water for a chill treat without the kick.

** *You can totally leave agave out if you don't like your drinks sweet. But we say fucking go for it. You've earned it.*

HOUSE RULES

Check the dollar store for those tiny umbrellas, because people love that shit. Spent all your money on the rum? Act like you're too cool and make fun of the umbrellas. Stay smooth.

SIP ON SOMETHING COOL
BECAUSE DOMINOES CAN GET
FUCKING HEATED

10 fresh mint leaves
1 teaspoon sugar*
½ cup peach puree**
¼ cup bourbon
1 tablespoon lemon
or lime juice
Ice
2 cups sparkling water
Mint sprigs or sliced
peaches, for garnish

PEACH JULEPS

A good peach can go a long way, but the bourbon will take you that extra mile. Sip on this cool cocktail and seize your summer.

1 Add the mint leaves and sugar to the bottom of a big pitcher or jar and mash them around with the back of a spoon to try and break down the mint a little bit. Add the peach puree, bourbon, and lemon juice and stir that shit around.

2 Pour this mixture into 4 ice-filled glasses. You can strain it if you want, your call. Add the sparkling water to each glass and garnish with some mint sprigs or peach slices if you are trying to act fancy.

The sugar will kinda exfoliate the mint and help release all that mint oil and other badassness we're looking for.

** *Just throw a ripe peach in a blender or food processor and run that fucker until it looks smooth. Done. Don't try this shit with an unripe peach because it will be garbage. And if you forgot to remove the pit, congratulations. You now own a broken blender.*

WATERMELON-STRAWBERRY TEQUILA PUNCH

MAKES ABOUT
18 CUPS, ENOUGH
FOR A FUCKING
PARTY

This is a classier version than that jungle juice some of y'all drank in your younger years. Growing up is good but tequila is better.

1 big seedless watermelon (about 16 pounds)

4 cups chopped strawberries (about 1 pound)

½ cup lime or lemon juice

4 cups sparkling water

1½ cups tequila

1 tablespoon of your favorite liquid sweetener like agave syrup (optional)

1 Halve the watermelon lengthwise and scoop out all the flesh into a big container with high sides. You want to use this container again to mix everything up, so choose wisely or you'll have more dishes. Working in batches, unless is you have the biggest fucking blender of all time, puree all the watermelon up.

2 As you go, strain the watermelon juice through a fine-mesh sieve or some cheesecloth to get rid of all that grainy shit. Strain it into the big container from before. You should get about 12 cups juice.

3 Take 2 cups of that juice and throw it in the blender with the strawberries and lime juice. Puree that fucker until smooth. You can strain this shit too if you want, but we kinda like the strawberry bits in the punch so we just pour it right in the watermelon juice container. You do you.

4 Stick this in the fridge and only stir in the sparkling water and tequila right before you serve. If it isn't sweet enough because you got some garbage fruit, then stir in the agave. Serve cold with plenty of ice or frozen fruit to keep it cold.

PARTY PLAYBOOK ✕✕✕

A FESTIVUS FEAST

During the holiday season, you gotta fucking eat. No matter what you celebrate or when you celebrate it, these recipes will be perfect to diffuse whatever inevitable family drama arises when people get together once a year to share a table. Fucking family . . .

MULLED SPIKED CIDER

This is some straight-up, right-after-some-caroling-and-sleigh-riding shit right here. Even if it doesn't snow where you're at, simmer up a pot of this holiday spiced goodness and you'll find it's always the season to be jolly.

5 cups apple cider
or juice*

1 orange, cut into slices

5 quarter-size slices
fresh ginger

3 cinnamon sticks

¼ teaspoon ground
allspice**

1 cup rum or bourbon***

1 In a large pot, combine the cider, orange slices, ginger, cinnamon sticks, and allspice and bring to a simmer over medium heat. Simmer for 4 minutes, add the rum, then turn off the heat.

2 Let this sweet winter bastard cool for a few minutes, then fish out the orange and ginger slices and the cinnamon sticks. Serve hot.

Just grab what looks legit. We like unfiltered apple juice, which is usually labeled "cider" depending on where you're at. Don't grab hard apple cider though, that shit is way different.

*** Allspice is not a suicide-style blend of spices; it's a berry with a confusing-as-fuck name. It is in a lot of Caribbean food and should be right next to the rest of the spices in the store.*

*** Driving the sleigh tonight? You can leave this out.*

MAKES A LITTLE
OVER 9 CUPS,
ENOUGH TO GET
10 TO 12 BUZZED
OR 4 TO 6 PEOPLE
LIT THE FUCK UP

SPARKLING WINTER CITRUS AND GIN PUNCH

2 bottles (750ml each) champagne or sparkling wine*

1 cup fresh grapefruit juice**

½ cup fresh blood orange or navel orange juice***

1¼ cups gin

1 cup sparkling water

¼ cup agave syrup or other syrupy sweetener****

Ice

Grapefruit slices, orange slices, and sprigs of mint or rosemary, for the punch bowl

This punch will have you seeing lights long before the ball drops on New Year's. Just make sure you've got some grub lying around or you might see some friends drop first.

_____

1 Chill everything for a couple of hours before throwing the punch together.

2 Pour the champagne, fruit juices, gin, sparkling water, and agave into a big-ass container like a punch bowl or a giant jar and mix well. Serve right away with plenty of ice. Float grapefruit, orange, mint, and rosemary in the punch bowl to make that shit extra special. Be prepared for guests to be sleeping it off at your place.

The sparkling wine does not need to be fancy shit. Anything will do. Also, just make each of your friends bring a bottle and save some cash as the host. Done and done.

*** About 3 large grapefruits.*

**** About 2 large oranges.*

***** Want to make your agave extra swanky? Add a tablespoon of water to it and bring it to a simmer on the stovetop. Add 2 sprigs of rosemary and 10 mint leaves and simmer gently for 3 minutes. Turn off the heat and let that shit cool. Pick out the herbs and stir this into your punch for extra flavor. Or don't, who gives a shit. Whatever.*

BLACKBERRY-MINT SPIKED LEMONADE

MAKES ABOUT
6 CUPS, ENOUGH
FOR 2 PEOPLE
LOOKING TO GET
LIT OR 4 REGULAR
FOLKS

This lemonade is a real game changer. So much so that you might never go back to that bottled shit in the cold case. Hate blackberries but like liquor? Try out the High School—Style Hard Lemonade on page 198.

2 lemons, chopped into chunks

15 large mint leaves

¼ to ½ cup sugar*

2 cups fresh or frozen blackberries

4 cups water

¾ cup bourbon**

1 Throw the lemon chunks, mint, ¼ cup sugar, blackberries, and water into the blender and let it go until everything is chopped the fuck up, about 1 minute. Use a fine-mesh strainer/sieve or some cheesecloth to strain out all the chunky bits when you pour it into a pitcher. Mix in the bourbon and taste that shit. Add the rest of the sugar if your blackberries aren't helping sweeten that fucker up as much as they should.

2 Serve it up cold or over ice and get ready for some adult-level Kool-Aid mouth. OH YEAH.

The amount of sugar you add will depend on how sweet your berries are. Try the lower amount first and then up that shit if it still tastes too tart to you.

** *Optional, but please.*

HOUSE RULES

Don't water down your punch by dumping a shitload of ice cubes in there. Those little bastards will melt quick and dilute your drink. Instead, add frozen fruit to make that shit look classy. A cheaper option is to freeze a couple inches of water in your Bundt pan (see House Rules, page 187) and stick that ice ring in your punch bowl. That shit will melt much slower than cubes and look way more badass.

HIGH SCHOOL–STYLE HARD LEMONADE

5 cups water

½ to ¾ cup sugar*

¾ cup lemon juice (about 6 lemons)

Juice of ½ lime

½ cup vodka, or more if reasons**

Lemon wedges and mint sprigs, for garnish

* Yeah, without all the sugar it's really just sour fucking water.

** 21 and up motherfucker. No ID? Replace this with water.

This takes us back to drinking that premade, bottled shit in the grocery store parking lot. But not like high schoolers ever drink . . . that would be illegal.

1 In a medium pot, bring the water to a boil over medium-high heat. Add ½ cup sugar and simmer that shit over low heat for about 5 minutes. Make sure to stir it on the regular. The sugar should be all dissolved in the water with no little fucking grains rolling around in there.

2 Remove from the heat and stir in the lemon juice, lime juice, and vodka. Let it cool until it is around room temperature. Put the lemonade in the fridge to cool down all the way in some kinda container or an old juice bottle. Taste and add the rest of the sugar or more vodka if you need that shit.

3 Serve with lemon wedges and some sprigs of mint if you want it to look fucking impressive.

HOUSE RULES

Leave permanent markers out next to your cups so guests can write their names or draw some shit labeling their cup. Otherwise watch a dozen people blow thru 100 cups in 30 minutes like FUCK THE ENVIRONMENT.

WHEN LIFE GIVES YOU LEMONS
THROW A FUCKING LEMON PARTY

PARTY PLAYBOOK
✗✗✗

BACK PORCH
SUMMER SUPPER

These dishes are a cool combo for warm summer nights. This is the perfect blend of refreshing flavors to fill you up on the inside even if you're breaking a sweat on the outside. The back porch is optional so feel free to eat in front of the AC.

SANGRIAS

Nothing says "party" like a big-ass pitcher of sangria. If you also happen to have activities at your party, maybe make that shit a moderate pitcher of sangria. Because nothing says "bruises" faster than sangria-fueled failed piñata swings.

RED SANGRIA WITH WINTER FRUIT

1 In a big container or pitcher, stir together the wine, brandy, orange juice, and fruit. (Don't stop and peel the fruit. Just throw it all in there.) Stick this in the fridge to chill for at least an hour or as long as overnight.

2 When it's time to get down, add the sparkling water and serve chilled with all the fruit still floating around.

* Use a red wine that is nice and cheap, but not so superdisgusting that you wouldn't drink it without fruit. Does the tag say it tastes like it already has some fruit in it? Cool, just grab that shit.

1 bottle (750ml) red wine*

½ cup brandy (or just leave it out if you think brandy is the fucking worst, bc honestly it kinda is)

½ cup orange juice

2 oranges, sliced into rounds

2 limes, sliced into rounds

1 apple, cut into slices

2 cups sparkling water or club soda

WHITE SANGRIA WITH MIDSUMMER PEACHES

1 In a big container or pitcher, stir together the wine, brandy, and fruit. (Don't peel the fruit. Just throw it all in there.) Stick this in the fridge to chill for at least an hour or as long as overnight.

2 When it's time to get down, add the sparkling wine or water and serve chilled with all the fruit still floating around.

* You want a white wine that's a little sweet but not syrupy and disgusting. Does the tag say it tastes like it already has some fruit in it? Kickass, just use that. The options in the wine aisle can be enough to induce a goddamn panic attack, so just keep it simple.

1 bottle (750ml) white wine*

½ cup brandy (or just leave it out)

4 white or yellow peaches, cut into slices

1 lemon, sliced into rounds

½ cucumber, sliced into rounds

1 bottle (750ml) sparkling white wine* or 2 cups sparkling water

MICHELADA

A little bit spice, a whole lotta beer, make one pretty fucking awesome drink.

4 cups of your favorite light beer*

¼ cup lime juice

2 teaspoons of your favorite taqueria-style hot sauce

1 teaspoon soy sauce or tamari

FANCY RIM (OPTIONAL)

1 tablespoon sea salt

1 teaspoon chili powder

½ lime, plus lime wedges

1 Mix the beer, lime juice, hot sauce, and soy sauce or tamari in a large container.

2 For the optional fancy rim: Grab a plate and mix the salt and chili powder together. Run the lime-half around the rims of 4 glasses. Turn each glass upside down on the plate and twist that motherfucker around until the chili salt sticks to the lime juice.

3 Pour the michelada mixture into the glasses and serve with a wedge of lime.

Don't bother with any fancy shit here. Just get a nice, affordable cerveza that you don't hate.

STRAWBERRY-CUCUMBER SMASH

This isn't just some sloppy slushie. No, this is a fucking shot of strawberry with a kick of cucumber and a hint of mint, which makes this simple smash a one-way ticket to no-frown-town.

½ cup strawberries

6 slices (¼ inch thick) cucumber

12 fresh mint leaves (optional)*

½ cup gin**

1 to 2 teaspoons of your favorite liquid sweetener like agave syrup

Ice

½ cup tonic or sparkling water

1 Grab a big-ass jar with a tight-fitting lid. Throw in the strawberries, cucumber, mint (if you're using it), gin, 1 teaspoon agave, and a big handful of ice.

2 Shake the ever-living fuck out of it until the gin looks all pink and lovely and the mint is beat to shit. Were your strawberries not supersweet? Got a bunk batch at the store? Just add a little extra agave and shake again.

3 Grab 2 glasses and throw in a couple ice cubes and the tonic. Strain the smash into each glass, making sure all the pulpy shit stays out. Serve right away before you accidently down both drinks yourself and have to start the whole fucking thing over before anyone notices.

* Optional, but who the fuck doesn't like mint? Ants, that's who.

** Better with it, but optional.

1 gallon water

8 black tea bags

¼ to ½ cup maple syrup*

2½ cups whiskey**

½ cup orange juice

⅓ cup lemon juice

Ice

Orange and lemon slices,
for garnish

SPIKED CITRUS ICED TEA

Summer party planned and it's hot as fuck?
Pull yourself together, find some shade,
and kick back with this spiked tea.
Guaranteed to refresh your attitude and
show your BBQ guests that you've got shit
handled. Even if you don't.

1 In a large pot, heat the water over medium-high heat until you see bubbles forming on the bottom. You don't need to fucking boil it. Turn off the heat and add the tea bags. Let them chill out in the hot water for about 5 minutes. You know, steeping and shit.

2 Pull the bags out and add the ¼ cup maple syrup, the whiskey, and citrus juices. Stir and taste. If you like it a little sweeter, just fucking add some more syrup.

3 Let the tea sit in the fridge until it's cool. Serve this summertime staple with some ice and orange or lemon slices because then it looks classy as hell.

Maple syrup can be expensive, so feel free to sub it with whatthefuckever liquid sweetener you've got, like agave.

**Optional, but c'mon.*

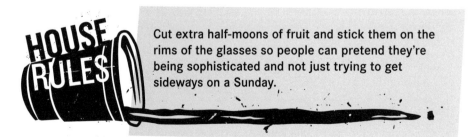

HOUSE RULES

Cut extra half-moons of fruit and stick them on the rims of the glasses so people can pretend they're being sophisticated and not just trying to get sideways on a Sunday.

THIS IS HOW TO GREET GUESTS

MANNERS MAKE FRIENDS, MOTHERFUCKER

A BLOODY MARY BAR IS ALWAYS A
SOLID FUCKING IDEA

NO BETTER WAY TO
START THE DAY THAN
WITH A BLOODY MARY

CAN'T REMEMBER THE LAST TIME
YOU HAD A BLOODY MARY THEN
IT'S BEEN TOO... HOLD UP.
WHAT... IN THE... FUCK?

LIGHTS OUT BLOODY MARY BAR

This is some DIY shit, so you really don't have to do much to get this bar going. Just lay everything out so people can make their own. Bonus: This takes up a lot of room so it looks like you worked a lot fucking harder than you did. Make a sign telling people what it is so you don't end up saying this shit out loud three times in a row and cursing the hell out of your brunch.

4 cups tomato juice or a veggie blend

1 tablespoon Tabasco sauce

½ cup lemon juice

1 teaspoon Bragg's,* soy sauce, or tamari

Black pepper

1 cup vodka

SALTED RIM
¼ cup flaky sea salt

1 teaspoon celery seed

1 teaspoon Old Bay seasoning**

ADD-INS
Lemon wedges, celery sticks, cucumber sticks, bell pepper sticks, dill pickle spears, green beans, prepared horseradish, carrot sticks

Ice

* WTF? See page 231.

** Old Bay is a supercommon spice blend that's added to shit like crab cakes, etc. If you can't find it by the spices at your store, just add paprika instead and move the fuck on with your life.

1 In a large pitcher or old glass juice jar, mix together the tomato juice, Tabasco, lemon juice, Bragg's, and a couple dashes of black pepper. Stir that shit around and taste. You can add the vodka now to make sure no one gets out of hand and drinks all your shit, or you can just put the bottle out and let people add it to their drinks themselves. Your call, but be honest with yourself if you know your friends can't hold their booze.

2 Set up the plate for making salted rims: On a small rimmed plate, mix together the salt, celery seed, and Old Bay seasoning. Take the rim of one of your glasses and stick it in there so it leaves a circle. This will show all the rookies at the party what the hell they're supposed to do.

3 To set up the bar, put out as few or as many of the add-ins as you want out. Have a bunch of glasses and ice ready and let people do the damn thing.

QUICK & DIRTY

If some of this shit looks familiar, that's because we covered it in our first book. Now just because you got this book, we couldn't assume you've got the first. If you do, high-fucking-five to you. But for those who don't, we're gonna give you a rundown on some Thug Kitchen basics so you'll be more comfortable in the kitchen than you are in the drive-thru.

BASIC POT OF BEANS

If you're new to this, you might see that our recipes call for a fuckload of beans. There's no shame in using canned, but throwing together a pot of beans is probably some of the easiest shit you can do in the kitchen. You just need to plan ahead and stay chill. The steps are the same regardless of what bean you're using; only the cooking time changes. Here are some guidelines, but trust your taste. The beans are done when at least five of them taste tender and are cooked through. Don't just trust one bean, it can be lying to you. So sample multiple beans. Keep simmering until you get there. Simple shit.

First, pick through the dried beans and throw out any that look fucked up, then rinse the winners. Put them in a big container and cover with a couple inches of water. They're going to swell up as they soak and you don't want those beany bastards sticking up out of the water. Soak them overnight or for at least 4 hours. This will help cut down on your cook time. (Throw them in the water before you leave for work and then they're ready to cook when you get home.)

When you're ready to cook the beans, drain off the soaking water and throw the beans in a big pot. Add a bunch of fresh water to the pot, about three times the height of the beans in the pot. Simmer, uncovered, until the beans are tender. Add a couple pinches of salt in the last 10 minutes of cooking for flavor. Drain away any extra liquid in the pot and store the cooked beans in the fridge or freezer until you're ready to use them. No can opener required. See, that wasn't so hard, right?

Here are some bean basics, but remember that shit really does change depending on how long you soaked your beans and also how old they are. So you've gotta have a little bean sense, but we can sense the force is strong as fuck with you. If you picked up some lentils or spilt peas, congrats, because you don't need to soak those fuckers at all. Otherwise just follow the directions above and you're in business. Beans and lentils tend to triple in size when you cook them, so if you want to end up with about 1½ cups of cooked beans (the standard can measurement), you want to start with ½ cup dried beans.

STANDARD COOKING TIMES FOR DIFFERENT BEANS

» Pinto beans: 1½ to 2 hours
» Garbanzo beans/chickpeas (same shit), kidney, and cannellini beans: 1½ hours
» Black, white, Great Northern, and navy beans beans: 1 to 1½ hours
» Black-eyed peas: 1 hour
» Yellow and green split peas: 30 to 40 minutes
» Green and brown lentils: 20 to 35 minutes

GRAINS

Cooking grains tends to be a lot quicker than cooking beans, but these fuckers are a little more high maintenance. But just like with beans, know that grains usually double in volume when you cook them so 1 cup of uncooked rice will give you 2 cups cooked. Use the following guides to get some grains going, just be sure to adjust that shit for how much you need for whatever you're making. If you ever end up with extra water in the pot when your grains are all done, just drain that shit off—don't keep cooking until your grains are all mushy. Also, if you run out of water and your grains aren't done, just pour a little more in. You're not going to fuck anything up. BELIEVE IN YOURSELF.

Brown rice

You might think this is some hippie health food, but it brings way more nutrition and flavor to the table than white rice. We always have a big pot of cooked brown rice in the fridge, and your ass should too. If you're still giving this motherfucker the side eye, try out the short-grain variety (below). That nutty, delicious motherfucker will make you forget white rice altogether. You can cook the long-grain variety in the same way, but that shit will take about 15 minutes longer and an extra ½ cup water.

MAKES 6 CUPS

BASIC BIG POT OF BROWN RICE

1 teaspoon olive or coconut oil (optional)*

2 cups short-grain brown rice

Pinch of salt

3½ cups water

1 In a medium saucepan, heat the oil (if using) over medium heat. Add the rice and sauté that shit until it smells a little nutty, about 2 minutes. Add the salt and water and stir. Bring to a simmer, then reduce the heat, cover, and let this very softly simmer until all the water is absorbed and the rice is tender, about 35 minutes.

2 Did you fuck up the heat and the rice is tender but there's still water? Just fucking drain it. Or the rice not done but all the water is gone? Just stir in more a little more water, turn the heat down, and keep going. Don't let some rice shake your game. YOU. GOT. THIS.

* This oil business is optional but it gives the rice a nuttier taste. Your call, motherfucker. Otherwise, just add the rice, salt, and water all in together and get simmering.

Couscous

This cooks quickly since technically it's a pasta, not a grain. Look that shit up if you don't believe us. Anyway, these mini motherfuckers will be ready in 10 minutes flat. Throw 1 cup couscous in a pot or a heatproof bowl with a pinch of salt. Add 1¼ cups boiling water, stir, and throw the lid on (or cover the bowl with a plate). No heat under the pot or anything. Let that sit for 8 minutes, then fluff the couscous with a fork and serve. Fucking done.

Millet

Yeah, this might look like birdseed, but it's cheap as fuck and deserves more love in the kitchen. It's kinda like a mix between quinoa and brown rice and worthy of a test run on your plate. Throw 1 cup of millet in a medium pot over medium heat and sauté it around until it smells toasty, about 2 minutes. Add 2 cups water and a pinch of salt and simmer that shit, covered, until the millet is tender, 25 to 35 minutes.

Quinoa

Some people cook this protein-packed grain like rice but treat it like pasta. To cook, bring 2 cups water to a boil in a medium pot with a pinch of salt, drop in 1 cup quinoa, and simmer, uncovered, until the quinoa is tender, 15 to 20 minutes. Drain away any water that's left.

OODLES OF MOTHERFUCKING NOODLES

Some recipes call for all kinds of different noodles and you don't have a goddamn clue why or how they're fucking different. We get it. So we've broken down some of the main noodles in the game so you can know when you can substitute that shit and when you need the real deal. Can't find what you need at the local market but really want it? Just find that shit on the Internet. But whatever noodle you pick, cook that shit according to the directions on the package. Those mother-fuckers know best.

Italian-style pasta

Anywhere we refer to "pasta" in the book, we mean the Italian-style stuff that lines the grocery store shelves next to the tomato sauce. It's made from hard durum-wheat flour, or semolina as it's sometimes labeled, which has more protein than your standard all-purpose shit. This means it's a little tougher and more likely to hold its shape and not turn to mush when you boil it. This shit comes in a ton of different sizes and shapes, so be sure whatever you pick is 1. the right shape to best hold on to the sauce your using, and 2. the right size if you're serving it with chunks of vegetables or beans. No matter what you choose, this pantry staple is not only delicious but affordable as fuck.

Whole wheat pasta

Just like the Italian stuff above, but with bit more fiber, protein, and B vitamins, whole wheat pasta is made of the same shit but processed in a different way. It still has the wheat bran and germ, which have both been removed from the traditional semolina pasta. This means it takes a little longer to cook, has a nuttier taste, has a little more grit to its bite, and can be a bit more expensive. You can totally use regular pasta in place of whole wheat if the budget is tight. Scared of trying something new? Try a larger pasta shape like penne first where you won't even fucking notice the slightly different texture.

Udon

These thick-ass wheat noodles come from Japan and are getting pretty popular. They cook up chewier and softer than Italian pasta and are more neutral in taste. They work great in soups and cold salads because they're easy to slurp and are damn tasty. They come in a variety of thicknesses and are either round or kinda flattened like fettuccine. You can find them dried in packages near the soy sauce in the store or sometimes sold fresh by the tofu if your market is fancy. Keep them stocked in your kitchen, because these bitches are about to go into rotation.

Soba

These badass noodles also come from Japan and are made from buckwheat flour, so they have a slightly rougher texture and nuttier taste than udon. Soba that is 100 percent buckwheat is pretty fucking expensive, so the more affordable shit has wheat flour mixed in, which makes them a little softer in texture. If you splurge on the pure buckwheat stuff, know that it's gluten-free. You can find them dried in packages near the soy sauce in the store.

Glass noodles/mung bean noodles

These tasty fuckers, which originated in China, have about a billion different names: glass noodles, mung bean noodles, cellophane noodles, bean threads. Whatever the fuck they're labeled, you can always recognize the bundles of very thin, translucent threads. They're made from mung bean starch (yes, that means they're gluten-free) and have a little bit of an elastic snap when you bite into them, but not in a weird way. Not sure you got the right shit? They're super see-through when cooked so you should fucking know by then. If you can't find them, you can use really thin rice noodles instead.

Rice noodles

These starchy sons of bitches are made from rice flour and are popular all over the world. Their texture is kinda elastic, but soft when warm, and they (predictably) sorta taste like rice. Like glass noodles, they have a billion names like rice sticks, rice vermicelli, mai fun, depending on their shape and thickness, kinda like Italian pasta. You can always tell you got the right shit though because they're white and kinda chalky in color. They're usually packaged in one big-ass bundle all folded up over themselves. They soften up superquick in hot water and are great stir-fried (think pad thai), in soups, and cold salads. You can find them dried in packages near the soy sauce in the store.

FAT RUNDOWN

When it comes to cooking and baking, not all oils are created equal or work for every job. Here's a quick cheat sheet for what to use where. No matter what you pick, heat your oils up until they shimmer and then get to cooking. Adding the oil and food to the pan at the same time means nothing's gonna cook right, so have some damn patience. If your pan starts smoking, it means your shit is too hot, so turn it down or use another oil because you straight fucked up. But the best lessons are learned the hard way, so don't let that hold you back.

AVOID

Right out the gate, DO NOT go buying some bullshit like these.

- **Vegetable oil**
- **Vegetable shortening** *(particularly if it is full of partially hydrogenated oils)*
- **Canola oil**

Most of these oils are highly refined and offer no nutritional trade-off. Grab something else and get your money's worth.

FOR LOW TO MEDIUM HEAT

- **Olive oil**
- **Unrefined coconut oil** *(this one tastes like coconut, stable at room temp)*
- **Any of the high-heat oils** *(see below)*

FOR HIGH HEAT

- **Refined coconut oil** *(no coconut taste, stable at room temp)*
- **Grapeseed oil**
- **Peanut oil**
- **Safflower oil**

FOR DRIZZLING, DRESSINGS, AND EXTRA FLAVOR

- **Extra virgin olive oil**
- **Toasted sesame oil**

BASIC SHIT TO ROAST AT HOME

Stop buying roasted bell peppers and garlic at the store because honestly you're just lighting your money on fire. And if you're buying canned beets, you must hate yourself because they're fucking disgusting. Just take 2 seconds to figure out how to do this easy shit on your own. Grab some foil and beets, peppers, or garlic, and get your ass in the kitchen.

Beets

Warm the oven to 400°F. Slice all the leaves and shit off the top of the beets, scrub them clean, but leave the skin on. Try to grab beets of the same size so they all roast at the same speed. Wrap them up in foil in a group and stick those blood-red motherfuckers in the oven (on a baking sheet in case they leak a little). Roast them until you can stick a fork in them with no resistance, 45 minutes to 1 hour.

When the beets have chilled out for a bit you can peel them. Hold one in a paper towel and use the paper towel to kinda rub the skin away. If you cooked those bitches long enough this will be super easy. Done. You can store them in a fridge for up to a week to throw into salads or use them right up.

If you like to eat beets on the regular, then don't stress about roasting them separate all the damn time. Next time you're baking any savory dish at 375°F or higher for awhile, just throw a foil packet of these guys in and let them bum a roast ride. Just keep an eye on them if the temperature is higher than 425°F, because they can dry out. Add a tablespoon of water to the packet while they're cooking if this shit happens.

Bell peppers

GAS STOVE: You can do as many of these as you have burners on your stove, but we usually stick to two at a time so our asses don't get overwhelmed. Set aside a large piece of foil for each pepper you're roasting. Place a bell pepper directly on the burner of a gas stove and turn the heat to high. Burn the ever-living fuck out of the skin of the pepper, rotating it until every side is blackened. This should take about 8 to 10 minutes for the whole pepper. Calm the fuck down, the more burned it looks, the better. When the pepper is burnt all the way around, place it in a piece of foil and wrap it up so that no steam can escape. It needs to cool down for at least 15 minutes, so go do something else and then come back. You can let this sit for awhile longer if you need to, so move on to other shit if you are busy in the kitchen.

When the peppers have cooled you'll be able to peel the burnt skin off the flesh no problem. Cut off the top of the pepper where the stem is still attached and start pulling off all the burnt skin. Yeah, your hands are gonna get dirty, but deal. Don't run the pepper under the sink thinking you're saving time because you'll lose that roasted flavor; don't fuck things up now. It's cool if you leave a couple black pieces here and there, it's all good. Once the peppers are cleaned, scrape out the guts and seeds, and then go make something badass with the flesh. You can do this shit a day or two in advance, just keep them in the fridge.

ELECTRIC STOVE: If you are working with an electric stove, you aren't getting left out but you do have our fucking sympathies. Heat up your oven to 400°F and line a baking sheet with some foil. Lay your peppers down on there, roast them for 25 minutes, turn, and roast them for 25 more, until they look all charred and soft. Wrap them up in foil just like the stovetop ones and follow the rest of the steps to peel them. Done and fucking done.

Garlic

Warm the oven to 400°F. Pull off all the extra layers of paper around a whole bulb of garlic. Slice the top ¼ inch right off the top to expose its innards. Pour ½ teaspoon of olive oil over the top and then wrap the bulb up in some foil. Roast this in the oven until all the cloves looks all golden and smell goddamn delicious, about 40 minutes. You can do a bunch of bulbs at a time in the same foil pouch thing if you're all about that garlic life.

Let it cool for a bit and then squeeze out as many cloves as you need. It will keep for at least 2 weeks in the fridge.

Know you'll want roasted garlic in the future but don't want to heat the oven up? Just follow the directions for roasting alongside other shit, like we wrote for the beets. Same shit applies.

BASIC RECIPES FOR STAPLES

Here are some basic recipes for making some simple shit for your kitchen.

Melting chocolate

There's a lot of places in the book (and in life if you're being fucking honest) where you need to melt some chocolate. If you do that shit too quickly or at too high a heat you'll end up with a bowl of grainy mud. So follow our instructions and dessert will be right around the damn corner where it should be.

METHOD 1, MICROWAVE: You can melt chocolate quickly and with the least amount of dishes by doing it this way. Slowly heat it in the microwave in 30-second increments and stirring in between until it is melted. The total length of time will depend on how much damn chocolate you are melting. Don't get crazy and try to do that shit in one big go because it will get fucked up. We promise. Just keeping stirring it every 30 seconds and heating it again until it is all melted and you'll be good. Swear.

METHOD 2, DOUBLE BOILER: No microwave? No problem. You get to build a double boiler like a fucking boss. Grab a medium saucepan and fill it with 2 to 3 inches of water. Throw an all-metal bowl on top of that and make sure the whole mouth of the pan is covered and that the water inside isn't touching the bottom of the bowl. Put this over medium-low heat and put the chocolate in the bowl. The steam will melt the chocolate, just keep stirring and fucking trust the method. When the chocolate looks all smooth, remove from the heat, and take off the bowl. Obviously the bowl is fucking hot so be careful, otherwise you are good to go.

Zesting citrus

When a recipe calls for zest, it wants you to get all the flavorful essential oils from the rind. You can do this shit two ways:

METHOD 1, GRATER: This way is easier but most likely to fuck up your knuckles. Grab your box grater or if you have a finer grater you use for nutmeg or Parmesan, grab that. Using the smallest side, gently scrape off the waxy outside colored layer of the citrus fruit. The white spongy layer (the pith if someone is trying to get fucking technical) is bitter and gross, so don't grate down past that. Keep going around the outside of the fruit until you get enough for your recipe.

METHOD 2, KNIFE/VEGGIE PEELER: This way takes a sharp knife or veggie peeler and a steady hand but we think you're fucking ready. Take your knife or peeler and shave off a thin-as-hell layer off the rind. Stick that on your cutting board, cut it into crazy thin strips, then dice those fuckers up so you get a minced-up zest. This method is awesome because you get more of the oils to stay in the skin where you need it, instead of all over your grater so you get more bang in your zest, which is all any of us really want in life.

Toasting Nuts

Throughout the book we ask you to use toasted nuts, so we thought we should walk you through that shit. Buying pre-toasted nuts is such a fucking waste of money, so do like we do and get toasted at home. There's two ways to do this, the stovetop, which is easier and faster, or in the oven, which is best for large batches. Whichever one you choose, DON'T. EVER. FUCKING. WANDER. AWAY. while you're toasting nuts. These oily little bastards burn in a hot second, so don't toast your money because you got distracted. Also, toast the nuts before you chop them up. The smaller the nuts, the easier they are to burn. Stay put until they're done and you'll be getting down on deez nuts in no time. GOT 'EM.

METHOD 1, THE STOVETOP: Heat a large skillet or sauté pan over a medium-high heat. Add the nuts in a single layer and then stir those sons of bitches frequently until the nuts turn golden brown and start smelling, well, nutty. Pour those fuckers out of the pan and onto a plate to cool. If you leave them in the hot pan, even off the stove, they'll keep cooking and probably burn. We're speaking from personal experience, so learn from our fuck-up.

METHOD 2, THE OVEN: Warm the oven to 350°F and pull out a rimmed baking sheet. Spread the nuts out in an even layer and stick that shit in the oven. Roast them for 5 minutes then pull them out, stir them around, then stick them back in for another 2 to 3 minutes to even out that roast. Depending on the nut, you might need to roast them for another 5 to 8 minutes, but until you get good at this shit, you'll wanna check every couple minutes so those bitches don't burn. They're done when they look all golden and smell all extra nut-like. Pull them out and pour them onto a plate to stop the cooking. Fucking done.

WHIPPED CREAM

MAKES ABOUT 1½ CUPS

1 You need some electric beaters or a stand mixer to do this shit. You're not strong enough to do this by hand, so stop fucking lying to yourself. Stick a bowl and the beaters in the freezer for 15 minutes to let that shit get chilly.

2 Take them out after 15 minutes and grab the milk from the fridge without shaking it up. Open up the can and scoop out all the thick white cream on the top half of the can and put it in the chilled bowl. (Leave that clearish liquid in the can and use it for a smoothie or something later.) Sift in the powdered sugar so that there aren't any chunks and add the vanilla if you want.

3 Now beat the fuck out of it on medium-high until it starts looking all fluffy and whipped cream-like, 1 to 2 minutes. Serve right away.

1 can (14 ounces) coconut milk, well chilled*

2 tablespoons powdered sugar

½ teaspoon vanilla extract (optional)

Put that shit in the fridge the night before so you know it's cold enough. You could do it an hour before you make this, but you'll fucking forget.

POPPING YOUR OWN POPCORN

1½ tablespoons
grapeseed or refined
coconut oil

½ cup popcorn kernels

What the fuck happened that made us all think we can't pop popcorn? Can you brush your teeth? Then you can make this shit all on your own without some steam-filled bag waiting to burn the shit out of your face.

1 In a large pot with a lid, heat the oil over medium heat. Add a couple kernels of the corn, cover, and shake it around every now and then. Once one of them pops that means your pan is ready. This might take up to a minute and a half.

2 When the oil is ready, add the rest of the kernels and cover that fucker up. (If you have a glass lid, you can use it here to supervise the hell out of your corn.) If they don't start popping within the first 30 seconds, turn your heat up just a bit. Soon it should start to sound like fucking firecrackers are going off in your kitchen as all the kernels start exploding. Shake the pan around every couple of seconds to keep those bitches from burning. It's like stirring without releasing all the heat. You'll smell it if that shit is starting to burn, so don't overthink this. Once you hear more than a couple seconds between pops, turn off the heat. See, that took no fucking time at all.

BASIC SHIT:
"OH FUCK, I HAVE TO BAKE" EDITION

Baking can be some scary shit, we get it. It's harder to taste-test along the way to make sure you haven't fucked up, and you're almost always planning on sharing it with other people who you don't want to piss off with terrible muffins. That shit can be stressful, but that's why we're here to help. Follow these guidelines and people will be asking you where you bought those brownies in no time.

YOUR OVEN IS FUCKING GARBAGE: Ovens are goddamn liars when it comes to what temperature they're actually at. You set that shit correctly but they're somehow 100 degrees hotter and your pie burns and everyone blames you. Fuck that, it's your shitty oven. The easiest way to fix this is to get an oven thermometer. They're less than $10 and just chill in your oven so you can read the temp off them and not your lying-ass oven. If you really want to get to know your oven, grab two oven thermometers and put them in different spots. This will help you see if there are any weird zones in your oven where it's hotter or colder than everywhere else. Yeah, apparently that's a thing too. So why the fuck are ovens so expensive again?

YOUR PAN IS CLINGY AS FUCK: You bake everything perfectly, it smells like a dream, but then you can't get that shit out of the pan. Listen, you need to grease and flour that motherfucker. Just put a little bit of whatever oil you're using for the recipe on a paper towel

and smear that shit all over the inside of the pan so everything is kinda shiny. Then throw a couple tablespoons of flour in there and shake that around until there's a light layer of flour on all the sides. Just shake out any extra still hanging out in there. Oh, you think parchment can save you? STILL. GREASE AND FLOUR IT. You'll never say "damn, I hate how easily my cake came out of the pan."

PATIENCE IS A VIRTUE, MOTHERFUCKER: Honestly sometimes you just have to wait for the good shit. When you're baking, cooling is as important as the actual baking process. Baked goods can change in taste and texture as they cool, so follow what the recipe says. Keep it in the pan as long as it recommends, and don't cut in all early and release that good heat. It will taste better in the end if you and baked goods just fucking cool it for a second. Just go look at some cat videos. Easy as that.

EVERYTHING IN YOUR CABINET IS OLD AND CRUSTY: Did you inherit your baking powder from your grandma? Throw that shit out. Seriously, if your cakes and breads aren't rising, then chances are your baking powder, baking soda, and/or yeast are old as hell and stopped working. Check the expiration dates and buy some recent shit. You can't get your cupcake on with some Bush-era powder. GODDAMN.

HEAVY HANDS WILL HURT YOU: We know you want to make sure your batter isn't lumpy, but sometimes you've gotta take it down a notch. Overmixing can cause baked goods to be all sunken in the center and gummy as hell. Follow the directions of your recipe and if it says "mix until *just* combined" that means "DO NOT OVERMIX THIS SHIT." Just stir until there aren't any big-ass pockets of flour and you're good. As long as you mixed all the dry stuff together well before you poured in the wet then you've got nothing to worry about. All those tiny lumps and shit will bake out, so just chill.

KEEP THAT SHIT COLD: When you are working with a dough that you want to be flakey (like pie crusts) you need to keep that shit cold. The more pockets of fat you have, the more flakes you'll have after you bake it, so do the damn thing right. To keep that oil from melting, you want to mix up all your dry ingredients and stick that shit in the freezer for at least 15 minutes or up to an hour before you cut in the fat. Keep the fat in the fridge but the dry stuff and the bowl in the freezer. We know kitchens get hot as fuck, so doing this extra step will keep your crusts looking right.

How to blind bake a pie crust

No, this isn't some kitchen magician shit. Blind baking a pie crust is when you cook the crust first without all the filling in it. You typically do this when you're making a no-bake pie filling like our Chocolate-Coconut Pie (page 181). We like to use the Extra Flakey Coconut Oil Crust (page 224) here, but you do you.

The idea of blind baking is that you fill the crust with about 1½ pounds of something heavy so that it doesn't get all saggy sided when you bake it and look like shit. We like to use some old-ass dried beans from the back of our pantry. You have to throw them out after, or save them for blind baking another pie crust, but their burrito days are over. It's a good way to use up those beans you bought 2 years ago and never fucking cooked. You can also buy ceramic or metal pie weights specifically for this shit so you can reuse them. Whatever you use, get that shit out and get baking.

» Position a rack in the lower-middle of the oven and heat up to 400°F.

» Roll out your pie dough and press it into your pie pan. Cut off any extra hanging over the edges and press the edge of the crust into a pattern: Pinch it around your pointer finger or make a pattern with a fork. You do you.

» Grab a large square of parchment paper or foil and line the inside of the crust on the bottom and all the way up the sides. Now dump in the beans or pie weights, making sure they are even all over the bottom of the pie and creep a little up the sides. Now throw that fucker in the oven and bake it until the crust is just a little golden, about 15 minutes. Pull that shit out of the oven.

» Now take out the parchment and whateverthefuck you had in it. And yeah be careful not to burn yourself because that shit did just come out of the oven. The bottom of the pie will still look kinda raw right now. You have not fucked up. Throw it back in the oven until the bottom is golden and the crust is browned but not burnt, another 7 to 10 minutes. If the edges of the crust are looking browned but the bottom still looks raw, take some foil and gentle cover up the edges to slow down the baking process so the bottom has time to catch the fuck up before the edge burns.

» It might have kinda puffed up a little while it baked, but that shit will deflate as it cools, so relax. Let this cool all the way to room temperature before you fill it.

IT'S ALIVE: All about yeast

Active dry yeast is the shit we call for in all our dough recipes and its not as scary as it sounds. You can find it in little packets in the baking aisle at the store, or sometimes in jars in the dairy case near the butter. If you know you will be using this stuff a lot save yourself some cash and get the jar, otherwise the packets are cool. Each packet, no matter what fucking brand you buy, has 2¼ teaspoons of yeast in it so that's what we call for in each of our recipes. If your yeast is old as fuck, your bread won't rise so when in doubt buy some new shit before you waste all that flour.

When you are letting your dough rise, you want to do it a warmish place with no drafts. We live in drafty ass places so we usually let our dough rise in the oven without any of the heat on and cover the bowl with a clean kitchen towel. Don't forget this shit is in there and start warming the oven though. You've been fucking warned. The dough will rise at slightly different rates depending on how warm it is in your kitchen so trust your eyes. If the recipe says "let it rise until it doubles in size, about an hour and a half" but that shit is huge by an hour then you are good to go. Baking with yeast is all about feel and less about recipes so trust your gut and get your ass in the kitchen.

2½ cups whole wheat
pastry or all-purpose
flour (or a mix of both)

2 teaspoons sugar

¼ teaspoon salt

1 cup refined coconut
oil,* cold enough to be
solid

¼ to ½ cup cold water or
nondairy milk

*We use the coconut oil shit
instead of shortening, but if
you have a tub you are trying
to finish out before making
the switch, you can use it
here. We won't judge.*

EXTRA FLAKEY COCONUT OIL CRUST

The best way to get a flakey-as-fuck pie crust is to use a bunch of fat, so here it is. Don't be afraid. Obviously pie isn't some everyday shit, so kick up your feet and know that you'll appreciate this fucker even more because you made it yourself. Now go take a lap.

1 This shit is easiest in a food processor, but you can totally do it by hand if you don't have one. Just follow the instructions in step 2. If you have a processor, go for it: In a large food processor, throw together the flour, sugar, and salt. Pulse it a few times so it gets all mixed up. Spoon in the coconut oil in nickel-size globs so it isn't just sitting there in a huge blob. Don't use your fingers because you don't want that shit melting yet. Pulse the food processor again a few times until the chunks of oil get all mixed in and it looks like chunky sand. Pulse in ¼ cup water until a dough comes together. If it still looks too dry, add enough of the remaining ¼ cup water, 1 tablespoon at a time, until it all comes together.

2 No food processor? You still can get pie, so life isn't totally fucking bleak. In a large bowl, whisk together the flour, sugar, and salt. Spoon the coconut oil into the flour in globs about the size of a dime. Your hands will melt that shit, so use the damn spoon. Use a big fork and break those fuckers up further into the flour so when you are all done it looks like rough, shitty sand. The smaller your oil globs, the flakier your dough, so take a fucking minute and do this shit right. Slowly stir in ¼ cup water and mix it up until a shaggy dough forms. If there's still way too much dry flour add enough of the remaining ¼ cup water, 1 tablespoon at a time, until a dough comes together.

3 No matter how you made your dough, when that shit is all mixed up, divide it in half and press each half into a small fat disk. Wrap each in plastic wrap and throw those bad motherfuckers into the fridge to chill at least 1 hour before you get going, or up to 3 days.

4 When you are ready to go, roll a disk out on a well floured surface and throw it in your pie pan and bake according to whatever fucking recipe you are using.

OLIVE OIL CRUST

This dough comes together in a fucking sec and is perfect for savory shit like our Cherry Tomato Galettes (page 153). Honestly you probably have everything you need to make this in your pantry right now. No excuses. Don't need both crusts? Halve the recipe or stick that shit in the freezer until you need it again.

MAKES ENOUGH
FOR 2 STANDARD
PIE CRUSTS

3 cups whole wheat pastry or all-purpose flour (or a mix of both)

½ teaspoon salt

½ cup olive oil, well chilled*

1 to 1¼ cups cold water or nondairy milk

We like to get the oil cold enough so it looks kinda milky, because it makes the crust a little flakier. But if you're in a hurry, just fucking forget about getting it cold.

1 In a large bowl, whisk together the flour and salt. Slowly pour in the olive oil and mix it up so there are little globs of oil about the size of lentils all through that shit. Slowly stir in 1 cup of water and mix it up until a shaggy dough forms. If there's still too much dry flour, add enough of the remaining water, 1 tablespoon at a time, until a dough comes together. Pat that into a ball shape and light rub another tablespoon of oil over the outside.

2 Divide the dough in half and press each half into a small fat disk. Wrap each in plastic wrap and throw those bad motherfuckers into the fridge to chill at least 1 hour before you get going, or up to 3 days.

3 When you are ready to go, roll a disk out on a well floured surface and throw it in your pie pan or on a baking sheet and bake according to whatever fucking recipe you are using. Done.

4 cups all-purpose or
whole wheat pastry flour
or a mix of the two
flours, plus more for
rolling out

½ teaspoon salt

1¾ cups warm water*

2¼ teaspoons active dry
yeast**

½ teaspoon sugar

2 tablespoons olive oil

EVERYDAY PIZZA DOUGH

This is our go-to dough for all our pizzas
(pages 118 to 124) and focaccia (page 60).
Fuck, you could even make cinnamon rolls
out of it if you got a little creative.
What's great about it is that you don't have
to knead this yeasty motherfucker for very
long, so you get all of tastiness with a
lot less of the work. Boom. If you are
making pizza, just throw on your toppings,
brush some olive oil on the crust, and bake
that shit at 475°F on a baking sheet until
the crust is golden, 10 to 12 minutes.

1 Whisk the flour and salt together in a big bowl and set it aside.

2 In a small glass, mix together the warm water, yeast, and sugar
and wait a couple minutes and see if the glass looks kinda foamy
at the top. If nothing fucking happens, then your yeast is old as
shit and died so you need to get some new stuff. RIP.

3 When the yeast is ready to go, pour that whole glass into the
flour bowl and stir it together until a shaggy dough comes
together. Still got a ton of flour hanging out in the bowl? Add a
little bit more water, up to ¼ cup more, a tablespoon at time until
there are no more piles of dry flour. This shit depends a lot on
how much moisture is in the flour, so it changes all the time.
SCIENCE! Knead the dough for a couple minutes until a smooth
ball comes together. (WTF is kneading? See page 228.) Rub the
olive oil over the dough and put it in a bowl. Cover that shit with a
clean kitchen towel and let it rise someplace that isn't too cold or
drafty until it's about doubled in size, about 1½ hours. (Fig. 1)

4 When it's all big and ready to go, punch it down to let some of that gas escape and just knead that shit a couple more times to get it back into a ball shape. (Fig. 2) At this point you can divide the dough in 4 equal parts and roll out the dough to make your pizzas, or throw the dough in a zip-top bag and stick it in the fridge for the next week. Just let it warm back up to about room temp before trying to roll it out after it's been in the fridge.

5 To roll out the dough, throw some extra flour out on your counter and pat some on your rolling pin. (No rolling pin? Go fucking get one and stop trying to use a wine bottle. It won't end well, trust us.) Roll your dough out into a circle-ish shape about ¼ inch thick.

* Like the temperature of tea that you could tell used to be warm but has been sitting out for a couple minutes.

** Or one ¼-ounce envelope of yeast.

Fig. 1

Fig. 2

HOW TO KNEAD

There are plenty of videos out there that show you how to do this but we are here for you if the power is out.

1 Sprinkle some flour on a big, clean nontextured surface like your countertop (if that shit isn't tile), your kitchen table, or a cutting board. The flour will keep your dough from sticking so even though it's kinda a big fucking mess, just do it. Plop the dough out onto the floured surface and sprinkle some more flour on top of it.

2 Now it's down to the real shit. Push the dough down and out and away from you using the heels of your hands. Kinda like those old-timey cartoons when you see them using a washboard if that makes any fucking sense. This is stretching out the gluten strands of your dough so when that fucker rises in the oven it can stand up instead of just collapsing back in on itself, so yeah, it's important.

3 Fold the dough in half, kinda turning it a quarter-turn clockwise toward you as you do it. Then press out again, and keep going for about 3 minutes. Yeah, that's a long fucking time, but a lot of recipes call for 10 to 15 minutes, so you're fucking welcome. Sprinkle it with a little more flour if it starts sticking to your surface as you knead.

4 Continue kneading until the dough comes together in a sort of smooth looking ball, 4 to 5 minutes total. Coat it in olive oil so it doesn't dry out while it rises and then let it do its thing all covered up while you clean up the flour you got all over your fucking kitchen. Check your ass, because you always end up with a weird flour handprint on there, trust us.

LAZY PASTRY BAG SHIT

Sometimes things just look better when you pipe them on, but most of us don't have a pastry bag. So this one is for us lazy folks who like good-looking shit. You can use this to frost a cake, pipe the filling for our Deviled Chickpea Bites (page 64), make the Butternut Squash Queso-ish Dip (page 46) look fancy as hell on a plate on nachos (page 74), or whatever the fuck you can think of. If the filling is hot, let it cool a little before you throw it in the bag so it doesn't melt the plastic.

Otherwise pipe your fucking heart out.

1 Spoon whatever you're piping into a large ziplock bag and kinda tilt it so all that shit goes into one of the bottom corners. Don't seal the bag; just twist it so that all the air comes out.

2 Now just cut off the corner of the bag and gentle squeeze the filling out of the hole onto whatever the fuck you are using it for, like it's icing on a cupcake. It's way fucking easier than it sounds. You can cut the hole larger or smaller depending on how you want that shit to look, but about ¼ inch is a safe bet if you have no clue what you're doing. You cut the hole way too big and it looks like garbage? Just scrape that shit out and into another bag and start again. Easy as hell.

SPICE STAPLES & PANTRY BASICS

Here we piled together a list of the simple shit you need to be able to cook like that badass we know you are. We know it looks kinda long, but trust us, you'll use all of it if you're cooking like you should. This is basic grocery store shit, so you shouldn't have to change up your shopping routine to keep your eyes peeled for this stuff. Now make a list, get your ass to the store, and be nice as fuck to the cashier. They deserve it.

If you're able to keep most of this at your place, you'll always be able to make something to eat even if the fridge is looking bare. Don't stress because you can't get this all at once because money is tight. It takes time to get your cabinet game on lock, so be patient with yourself and keep a running list of what you need on your cell. That will: 1. keep you from buying four things of cinnamon in 2 months (been there), and 2. help you make sure you're grabbing exactly what you need when that sale hits.

BASIC DRIED HERBS AND SPICES

» One good, all-purpose, no-salt seasoning blend
» Basil
» Black pepper
» Cayenne pepper
» Celery seed
» Chili powder
» Cinnamon
» Cumin
» Garlic powder (granulated garlic is cool too)
» No-salt yellow curry powder
» Onion powder
» Oregano
» Salt
» Smoked paprika
» Thyme

PANTRY SHIT

» Olive oil (we use extra virgin olive oil everywhere it says olive oil in here because we love that shit)
» A neutral-tasting oil (peanut, safflower, or grapeseed)
» Soy sauce or tamari
» A nut/seed butter you prefer (peanut, almond, tahini, whatever)
» Rice vinegar
» One other vinegar you prefer (apple cider, balsamic, white wine, whateverthefuck you find)
» Your favorite grain (short-grain brown rice for the motherfucking win)

» Your favorite pasta
» Canned low-sodium diced tomatoes
» Your favorite dried and canned beans (keep both stocked for when you're in a hurry and when you can take your time)
» Your go-to flour (whole wheat pastry, all-purpose, rice, whatever your favorite shit is)

VEGETABLE BASICS

» Yellow onions
» Garlic bulbs
» Carrots
» Some kind of leafy green like cabbage, spinach, or kale
» Frozen green peas

WTF IS THAT?!

NOOCH

Nutritional yeast, or *nooch* if you're cool like that, is some real throwback shit. It's deactivated yeast sold in flakes that makes everything taste kinda cheesy. It's packed with B_{12}, folate, selenium, zinc, and protein. You can find it in bulk bins at some grocery stores, near the soy sauce sometimes, and on the Internet. It is not the same thing as brewer's yeast, which you don't ever fucking need.

BRAGG'S LIQUID AMINOS

Yeah, more hippie shit. It tastes and looks a lot like soy sauce but has a little something extra that's hard to explain. It's fucking delicious though, and totally something you should keep on hand. You can find this sauce near the soy sauce or vinegars at most stores or, again, on the goddamn Internet.

LIQUID SMOKE

This shit does exactly what you think it does: adds a smoky flavor to whateverthefuck you are cooking up. It's made by collecting the smoke from burning wood chips, and adding a little water to the mix. It adds a shit-ton of flavor but is easy to overdo, so be careful when you're measuring that shit out. Sure you can make this yourself if you're crazy about that DIY shit, but just buy it and save yourself the work. It's in a bottle near the BBQ sauce at the store so stop thinking you can't find it. It's there.

TEMPEH

This shit is fucking delicious but doesn't sound that way outta the gate, we get it. It's a brick made of fermented soybeans and because it is fermented, sometimes it might look like it has some mold on it, but just fucking go with it. It adds a great texture and kinda nutty taste to whateverthefuck you are cooking. One cup of tempeh has 30 goddamn grams of protein in it, so you have no excuses to not try it. You can find it in the fridge of a well-stocked grocery store and the Internet.

TOFU

Everybody knows what this is, but most people have no fucking clue how it's made or how to fucking cook it. Tofu is made from soy milk that has been curdled, the liquid drained away, and the remain solid stuff is molded into bricks. By itself it can be soft and have no fucking flavor, so think of it more as something that needs to be fucking seasoned rather than as an ingredient that's bringing any flavor to the table. One cup of tofu has 20 grams of protein, is rich in calcium and iron, and is cholesterol-free, so stop being afraid and try this fucker out at home. You can find it in the fridge packed in water and in aseptic containers near the soy sauce at the store.

PANKO BREAD CRUMBS

Panko is much lighter than traditional bread crumbs and is broken into large, coarse flakes rather than tiny-ass sand-looking pieces. The crumbs are used to coat all types of fried and baked shit because they stay crisper longer than most bread crumbs. You can grab a box of these fuckers somewhere near the soy sauce in your grocery store or near the rest of the bread crumbs.

THANKS

MH: To my family for their love and support; to Matt and Diane, my other two Musketeers; to Brown for showing me how to hustle; to Ravi for those what-the-fuck-just-happened nights; to Jon and Christine for showing me the meaning of hospitality; to Patrick for inspiring me to keep learning; to Brian for encouraging me to keep laughing; to Lucien for holding down the fort; to Kari for showing me the beauty in pain; to Jim for the sage advice and memories of my mom; to Chris for the endless words of encouragement; to Phoenix for existing in all her glory; and to all the readers motivating us to keep fighting and stay hungry. I love all y'all motherfuckers.

MD: To my family for always leaving second helpings; to VJ and Rebecca for their easy laughs and sound advice; to Jade for all the texts and schemes; to Peter for always having faith; to Maya for being so brave; to Max because I stole your damn joke; to Alex for always lending a hand; and to Koren for reminding me to take a damn break. Thanks also to everyone I worked with at the grocery stores in SD and LA. Even if we never hang, know that I miss you motherfuckers more than I can ever say out loud. And lastly, thanks to every single one of you who shared a post, liked a photo, cooked a dish, and spent your hard-earned money on the things we've made. It's a fucking privilege to feed and entertain y'all and we'll do it forever if you let us.

And none of this could've been possible without the crew at Rodale—Dervla, Jeff, Rae Ann, Mary Ann, Yelena, Aly, Susan, Brent, Evan, Nancy, Chris, Sara, and Mollie. To Lauren for being such a fucking boss, along with Richard and Kim at Inkwell; to Sally at Stroock for the muscle; to the whole crew at UTA; to Tim at Process Media for trusting our silly shit and Dan for fully embracing it; to Hayley for the style and laughs; to Nick Smith for sousing his heart out; to the Spork Sisters Heather and Jenny for giving us people to look up to; to Ian and Megan for sharing space and laughs; to everyone who partied on this book's behalf—y'all made this look good. And last but not least, to Mr. Nick Hensley-Wagner, your incredible art contributions make this book worth looking at. Thanks to all of you for all your hard work, early mornings, late nights, infinite patience, and relentless enthusiasm. We owe y'all some fucking drinks.

Underscored page references indicate sidebars. **Boldface** references indicate photographs.